Jewels of Truth

The Wayfarer of the Soul
Volume 2

Ivan A. Pozo-Illas, a.k.a. Atrayo

iUniverse, Inc.
Bloomington

Jewels of Truth
The Wayfarer of the Soul, Volume 2

iUniverse books may be ordered through booksellers or by contacting:

iUniverse
1663 Liberty Drive
Bloomington, IN 47403
www.iuniverse.com
1-800-Authors (1-800-288-4677)

ISBN: 978-1-4620-5899-0 (sc)
ISBN: 978-1-4620-5900-3 (e)

Printed in the United States of America

iUniverse rev. date: 11/22/2011

I dedicate this next volume of "Jewels of Truth" to the Holy Spirit my Oracle within. Although this is a small book with another batch of 365 all original spiritual wisdom statements and proverbs. I am still grateful for the role and source of all this inspiration that stems from within my Divine being. Without my Angels I would have not realized this God given gift and then developed it as an ability. I am truly humbled before thee our God(dess).

For those I clearly care about in this world, which goes out to my immediate family. Especially the continued central supporting role my mother Sonia plays in this life for me. Although I am still unknown she encourages me to pursue what I seek in earnest. So far this has been the wholeness of my being and "Jewels of Truth" as it has continued to set me free via inspiration. Amen.

Contents

Introduction

Here we are at another Volume of "Jewels Of Truth" bringing my entire collection printed into circulation of 730 spiritual wisdom based statements. Although now as I am writing this next introduction I am really writing Volume 3 where my present count numbers at #958 of original material.

I am grateful for this ability to use automatic writing as a technique to articulate these inspired messages. That I receive throughout my common hours. These spiritual wisdom quotations and statements to the modern day proverbs are from a yearning to understand this world of ours that is always in flux. My first name of "Ivan" spelled backwards is "Navi" which I often muse means "Navigator". So with all this wisdom I have witnessed and shared here in these volumes. I hope in a innocent way to leave a bread crumb trail or a "Map of the Soul". In how to reach purity of being be it by grace or struggling with karma itself.

I try in these statements to be inclusive and have a universal bent from the angle I write this content. However if I fail I am still growing as a soul and I may have tended to criticize rather than to uplift. As those of you that have read Volume 1 of "Jewels of Truth: A Soul Odyssey Within". You'll recognize how my writing style has evolved over the years and how it continues to evolve for the better in articulation.

I am grateful for this gift and ability to put into words the essence of spirituality. That others may use not as a tool of separation but of remembering we are all one in the eyes of God.

Thank you for reading these words and messages I have furnished for the highest good in all of us.

The Journey Continues, Ivan A. Pozo-Illas.

AKA: Atrayo.

June 1st, 2009.

(Notice: These statements below were written by psychic automatic writing. Thus shared due credit goes to my Spirit guides and teachers as a Host of Angels. Who call themselves as a place holder name "Oracle" or my own slice of the "Holy Spirit".)

A

Action:

One does not change the world, the world changes you. It all depends how we flow with or against conformity. Do we stand out and act upon the truth or do we buckle and collapse into the homogeneous dust around us? There is a choice that is awkward, but also sublime. Or no choice at all that makes the decision on our behalf. Do we become or do we get acted upon? Do we allow the tempest within to shine or do we throw the drapes on this performance as a curtain call? What is our next move and the one after that? Do we become rigid or bend like the reeds in the wind to allow ourselves to be molded by the greatest artist within, we call God(dess) the creator. Amen.

—–

Half an attempt is no attempt at all. One must be willingly to stretch beyond their own comfort zone. Or risk failing more often than is necessary to achieve what was desired in the first place. A full attempt may fail in effort, but one has pushed themselves beyond what is known to them at that moment in time. Resulting in learning a lesson and personal growth for the next attempt to be even better than the first one. That is if the desired results are sensible and not unrealistic in nature to be achieved by sweat equity. By giving fully to an attempt one succeeds no matter the outcome. Due to the tenacity of the persons intent akin to a full sense of being earnest. The path is assured to those who are faithful to their own actions. Merely by balancing out what is before them by what can be achieved during those turn of events. Will keep your foot stable and your mind clear on where to proceed next. This is what is needed in order to execute upon your own actions well. Amen.

Addiction:

Any negative thoughts, words, or actions done by compulsion will cause strife and chaos in one's life. Those who are under such clutches of addictive responses will not find peace until they give in to the compulsive behavior. This is often a false De facto peace until another urge of temptation is elicited from within themselves. Only a great stirring of fear or love can dislodge such an addiction. All addictions are parasites to the mind, heart, and physical body. Where the only method to remove such a turmoil is by the honest permission of the addict. Until that moment arrives heartaches and insane behavior will prevail. Before the path of sobriety can be found, and begun for ones highest good. Remember the path to wholeness is never walked alone, their is always a multitude walking with you. Both in the seen and especially the unseen by all that is Holy and in Spirit in this life. Amen.

--

For those who partake of any sort of addiction in one's life. It is akin to entering a state of oblivion when acting out in such destructive behaviors or habits. Only a sincere awareness can lead one back to a better lifestyle that is on an even keel. Followed by a regime that provides a prolonged course to a personal recovery for the addict and any care givers in supporting roles. Only then will the first shoots of normalcy will begin to take root and eventually flower into a sturdy sapling. Keeping in check the environment and associates of the former addict in order to avoid a serious relapse. Minor setbacks are to be welcomed and expected because without them the addict isn't taking his or her own recovery seriously.

Those of you who shall act as the stewards of those in recovery from addictions. Where for your courage and vision in seeing your loved ones as whole again as not just people, but as souls. For your compassion will yield a greater personal satisfaction in your lives. No matter the apparent struggles or deemed lack of progress of those your aiding in recovery. You are the pillars for which the ones in recovery will stand upon with a renewed conviction. Yours will be the first fruits of glory for all those you've made relative degree's of impact in their collective lives. Amen.

———

For where ever a person empowers another person, object, or activity in such a manner for it to become eventually destructive. They immediately enter into a lifestyle that will only bring harm by a myriad tendencies of addiction. Thus becoming slaves to someone or something that once brought abundant pleasure, will now only bring misery. Where the short term gain's of self-medicating by an addiction will stunt your growth as a functional person. For a short term numbing of your emotional or mental anguish you will always sell yourself short.

Where the consequences will become a revolving door from fear to pain. A true form of double jeopardy will be brought on in all encounters that will remind you of your anguish of the heart.

In order to regain sobriety be careful not to replace one addiction for another. Which will only compound any hope of a real recovery. When on the path of healing truth will be painful but necessary. Consider the truth as a form of antiseptic in order to stabilize your wounds of the heart and mind. It will sting deeply at first but over time it will soothe your wounds.

Safeguard your sanity for without it during recovery one will only succumb to the same addiction your trying to escape. Be still in mind and heart and in doing so you shall have plenty of courage to spare. Amen.

--

The characteristics of addiction are many with just as many expressions. The main tendencies are that of a narrow mindset bent on filling a void in their life. Lifestyles that once were manageable become warped and dysfunctional. Secondary addictions can also appear thus complicating one problem with another. Where venting the excess stress becomes its own self fulfilling prophecy. Rigid attitudes of the addict take over forcing recovery away as an alternative to escape the pain and suffering. Before any person as an addict is to choose wisely to heal their obsession of addiction. They must emotionally realize that the very act of their self-destructive conduct is causing more pain. Than the original flight to the addicts short term high. From any pleasurable escape from the stresses of everyday life. No intellectual acknowledgment is ever enough to ween an addict from their course of personal destruction. Only the courageous role models willing to lend a hand as a support network of contacts. Can ever offer the addict a wholesome alternative to choose again not a pleasurable high. But to align themselves through a regime that cleanses the mind, body, and especially the heart. Of its own suffering into a place that is both stable and loving for themselves and that of their own loved ones.

Affection:

Material gifts be they financial or otherwise are not a replacement of a sincere intimacy in a relationship. Be it a parent to a child, between lovers, or a dear friend. Gifts have their place on special occasions in order to create kind memories lasting a cherished life. Tokens of appreciation however welcomed can not ever give a hug or the warmth of ones heart to another. Only by offering your presence abundantly will you gain the adoration you seek. If those who truly love you, will love your company more than your material gifts. Know this and you will avoid losing a lover, losing the respect of a child, and most of all losing your sense of self. Amen.

Angels:

We are all Angels of various orders of creation come to be reborn and some of us are diminutive to grandiose in spiritual stature. However we came to humble ourselves so that we may follow in the foot steps of the Divine Light of God. By doing so we gain an appreciation of what is Holy and what is clearly not.

Appreciation:

Why do we crave for love and appreciation as souls?

We are more than a singular spiritual entity of God's making. When we combine our interests with other beings of a like mind and heart we truly become alive. We can transcend our mere mortal shells into a splendor that only

God(dess) can offer us. We become one in a unified "Spirit of God" where such a harmony affords us the attributes of love and appreciation. In truth when we harmonize such qualities in ourselves and within others we become open vessels. Allowing our spirits to transcend the mundane into the sublime according to the "Will of God". Which constantly bathes our spirits in the rays of his glorious absolute Love. Amen.

Approval:

Those who seek approval from outside themselves will never truly find it. For true approval of one's identity comes from within your own soul, where God lives in you. Those who seek acceptance have a better chance of finding it outside themselves. Where respect may be earned but at a cost, whether deserved by dignity or by the fear of others. Acceptance from others is like vanity, it can be very fickle. Adoration is not meant to replace approval or acceptance. It is truly meant for those who are beloved.

Where do you find your grace?

Art:

The creative arts are very close to our soul. It is no wonder why the inner splendor of our spirit manifests so readily in our lives. Through both as art that is natural all around us. Or that is fashioned by mortal means of the creative spirit. Art is the substance of the ethereal mind and spirit cultivating a work into fulfillment. The essence by means of creative technique and style by order of genre comes from the talent. Nothing else is important, if a work of art is fair or abysmal it is all in the eye of the beholder critiquing the medium itself. The soul must express what it can not articulate. For if the soul can easily express itself than art would not be needed as a form of self-expression.

—-

Art is the greatest expression of the creative soul within all that is and will be. Art is a reflection of what is felt or what is being sought after in one's heart or mind. Art can be of beauty, and its works can appear beautiful to the beholder. However art isn't pinned down only to reflect the beauty in nature or of the human condition. Art can be political in nature if so desired, to various degrees of success or failure. In generations yet to be, which will be its inheritors for better or for worse. Art is our reflection of ourselves in how we choose to depict our reality by truth or falsehood. We are the wiser if we can appreciate the artist as much as the body of work of the art itself.

Ascended Masters:

Many Faiths and Religions have all manner of Prophets and Saints to uphold in devotion. Including to a degree their creator come to life on this Earth as a savior. No matter the persuasion or declaration of faith these souls are to be upheld as examples to follow. Not to follow solely by the dogma, creeds, or theology such a faith decree's to the exclusion of all else.

What I'm speaking to are the role models such people we have cherished on this Earth have left us in remembrance. They are the living embodiment of God having walked amongst our forefathers as ideals of virtue and benevolent service. In following such sacred men and women we honor not just their memory, but ourselves in the journey of this lifetime of ours.

Do not trip up your brother and sister by declaring how wrong they are by their faults. Show them that there is an alternate path, by their permission in living well and in a Spirit of goodness. Just as those we worship came to this Earth to teach us how to be noble souls before the presence of our creator. Amen.

Ascension:

Everyone wishes for a personal genie and their destined "Three Wishes" to fulfill their own version of glory. Perhaps the best wish of perfection sought can be to make no wish at all. Why make a wish for something that is already yours to begin with? Everything is yours already in God's Spirit, the method in claiming your highest good is the journey to Paradise. In whatever way you seek to make such a definition into a complete realization. The trick is the perception to such a total transition through the ultimate looking glass within your very own soul. That will fill one's being as a bridge between realities for a non-linear existence. That can remake a physical mortal being into a spiritual lucid immortal being of creation. Such a way of life can take one into a myriad of realities for the benefit of ones soul and for the service of many others by grace. Where those that are served with compassion will live on through him or her own's essence for all times. Amen.

Awakening:

Adversity is the greatest resistance known to us all where pain can spring forth. Much as how the Buddha spoke that pain is inevitable and suffering is optional. The paradox of pain is that it will make a person stronger for those who are able to endure. Making them hopefully wiser and astute as a soul in such a lifetime. The paradox of pleasure is if too much is experienced it will warp the senses corrupting the heart and mind. If either extreme of pain or pleasure falls upon the head of a person it will spoil their will and ruin their noble heart.

The truest path in order to experience this life is the middle way by means of moderation. Whereby walking the narrow path between both polar opposites one can achieve a wholesome resolve to live well. Such a narrow path of moderation is never straight or linear it will spiral one back and forth. Until a patience is developed that will allow one to walk by confidence in such a duty to self-realization.

Be calm, do not force such a process for it must be experienced within the mind, heart, and spirit. In order to fully understand the scope of ones unfoldment by means of service to oneself and especially of the world at large. Be gentle, but act with a firm hand and the way of compassion will be revealed to you. Speak the truth, but do so that allows all others to speak their truth as well. Observe the beauty all around you and the beauty within life will acknowledge you with many wonders. Let go of your troubles and your troubles will dissolve into the Holy Light of your good soul. Most of all Love deeply and unconditionally, but not as a zealot, but gently and firmly through the narrow path of moderation. There you will find your oasis awaiting for you in all its splendor. Amen.

--

The reign of Love across eternity echoes a life of wonder. Only those who are its true stewards shall achieve the internal majesty from within that unleashes the totality of God's being. By doing so one embarks on an odyssey that only the humble and brave could Imagine in a dream of dreams.

Dreams are not the means to such an awakening, but only a medium to the catalyst of such a path into an unfolding in your personal life. There are many paths to God(dess) as their are leaves on an olive tree, and yet still more. True Love is the guiding light from within the soul and the basis to be guided onto redemption from your personal miseries. That is only a stage of an unfolding story that spans the breadth of eternity. Let the rule of Love by unconditional terms guide you to your own personal paradise. Where life is one with you as in the Alpha and Omega creating beautiful opportunities where memories of grace shall be cherished in this one life and in the next. Amen.

B

Beauty:

Beauty should not always be assumed to be loving, safe, and benevolent by appearance sake. Since deception can lay waiting to trap the unsuspecting person, or worse take one's life entirely. Beauties allure is its ever so present seduction of the weak, it is mother natures way to attract and defend itself.

Beauty when found in nature can be also a chief reason why the lust of the flesh can take hold easily. Beauty can both reveal and hide its truer intentions depending on the motives of the beauty involved. The key is to know the disposition of the inherent nature of the beautiful, is it loving or is it dangerous?

--

What is Beauty?

Beauty has an inherent balance by its aesthetics. A symmetry of order that fills us with a sense of awe and appreciation. Beauty is living art whether by its contrast or gesture. It is a representation of the Divine in all of us. A sacred union of souls that transcends often our comprehension of its depths of magnitude. Beauty is what it is, wonder that is manifested!

--

Beauty is the tranquilizer of the soul.

Benevolence:

Life itself is an experiment to be a dynamic form living with depth so as to be experienced. No one person nor an institution fashioned by mortals can provide an absolute guarantee to anything of a rightful outcome. Only God's grace in harmony with the "Holy Spirit" can any sort of pristine nature take hold. Co-existence with the Divine adds an additional element to the soul that words fail to quantify. Only when our intent is in harmony with the mysterious "Will of God(dess)" can we begin to have a meaningful life. Of course the caveat here is a life of benevolent living leads into the "Will of God". Whether a person is unfaithful living in a secular fashion or a devout person with faith. Goodness trumps all the limitations a religious body can place on non worshipers via their viewpoint with exclusions of "This or That". Amen.

Bliss:

For those who seek "Bliss" without being ignorant. The path is not an easy one, however it is achievable by the gentle hands of grace within your own soul. To achieve this bliss through awareness one must surrender all that is vain and worrisome. By surrendering your viewpoint of being right versus being good, will allow you the freedom to experience bliss with abundance.

Be centered within that which is true and purest. Where your best guide is that of total love for all that is sacred and divine. Be aware that this path will undo your own vain human ego. By allowing a freedom where few can navigate without prejudice in their hearts. Amen.

Burdens:

The Lord our maker creator of Heaven and Earth. Will not allow life to be a function of futility for those who adhere to his being. Life has always consisted of burdens and trials. However the mortal life can be eased by an unconditional faith in one's creator of a most blessed life. Such a faith will not erase one's burdens. But it will give each one the strength and wisdom to surmount by grace and mercy their burdens and trials. Do not give in so easily to despair, have faith in your own personal deliverance by your own good works. Amen.

Business:

People of all sorts are to be considered as treasures. Not merely as a commodity of labor or as an asset class of property. Be it in the setting of a small business owner (manager) to that of a corporation or a government institution. Each individual has talents, has a family, has a life, needs to love(serve). Treating people respectfully will insure longevity for those seeking to herald long term projects of various kinds. People always come first otherwise the quality of your projects will diminish in capacity.

––

What I see as opportunity going unfulfilled, becomes an affront to human charity and commerce. That of under used, neglected, creative people who are full of promise and vibrant potential. But are not regarded for there true talents or worse discarded by woefully inadequate managers and administrators.

Such lost opportunities for growth and enterprise hurts morale. But seriously profits or charitable revenue are not given the chance to materialize. Thus a business or non-profit becomes an ignorant casualty of its own stupidity. Develop talent skillfully and with wise counsel and the wonders to come will astound the new and old alike, I promise you.

Change:

Before there is a great calm be it of a place or circumstance, there is always a great disturbance to follow it. This is how the cycle of change will function from the common to the extraordinary. Where events will transpire based on the intent of others or to the cause of natural movements moving at an internal tempo. One must not resist change that is restorative, however one should always be inclined to resist change that is destructive. As time passes from our mortal eyes lessons learned and forgotten will take hold. Be the wiser and keep your lessons alive, lest you repeat hardships that could have otherwise been avoidable.

Character:

In depth of human character there is always complexity. That begets the question of "Why and How so?" in regards to an individuals makeup as a person. This is where discretion and not being quick to judge will garner more truth. Than that of rash thinking of "So and So" a person akin to gossip. Be still and unravel the enigma of a person's motivations and their intents of who they truly are, in regards to their overall self-image personified. Such is the beginning to understanding such and such a person who is complex or otherwise full of depth of character.

--

Divine truths or laws are universal in scope and reach for they are expressed infinitely through all Life be it in spirit or in the flesh. Life long character building traits emphasize such a proof by the goodness of the soul on display by their deeds. Without prejudice nor order of magnitudes can the "Will of God" be impinged upon. Those entities that fully awaken spiritually often referred to as the "ascended masters". Are the ones that are keen in fulfilling the mandate of Heaven on this Earth of ours. Where their awareness leads them to be in a constant state of "Lucid Awakening". Forever in the present moment, mindful of not only their intentions, but the intentions of those men and women all around them.

We can act in kind, by being mindful of this present turn in our circumstances. We can not all be saints and ascended masters. However we can try to be like them in certain aspects that are righteous and well meaning to our peers. The Divine Laws are truly our spiritual inheritance in how we govern our lives and offer guidance to our loved ones. We can lead by a just example or fail to fully measure up to the standard of dignity set out by those we deem as both Saintly and Angelic. Amen.

Cheerful:

If laughter is medicine for the soul through the veins of our happiness. Than tears of joy is the washing away of misery built up over the years. That cleanses a person from the mind all the way to the heart. Do not keep sadness for too long in your company. Or you shall welcome its cousin tragedy into your life. Be mindful of the company you keep does not just apply to your social lifestyle. It also applies to how well you conduct your mind and heart in a right form of living.

However you may define such an act please treat yourself with dignity. For if you can not love yourself sincerely than who will? Your relatives, spouses, and friends will only care for you awhile. However they have their own lives to live and duties to fulfill. If you depend on their love alone to keep you going. Than you are cheating yourself from knowing the unconditional love that God and his Angels offer. To all who are open to them in life by thought and action. Keep a merry spirit not just for yourselves, but for the world at large that is always in need. Stay well in spirit and you shall inherit the "Kingdom of God" on Earth. Follow your truest love and all the riches in heaven are sure to follow. Amen.

Child of God:

In Heaven there is no error or sin, no wrong doing of any kind. Thus for all creations of God(dess) may enter paradise without any indignity upon them. All this is forgiven with unconditional compassion for all children of God. There is no need to judge your neighbor falsely, nor persecute them without witness to the point made above. Accept yourself as a Divine creation with a mortal guise, and relinquish all burdens that humanity imposes on you. Let go of these misleading traits so as to be who you truly were meant to be a blessed child of God. Amen.

--

What is this mystery we call God and of such as it is expressed through life? Well it is a splendor if one permits it to be in regards of their own willful temperament. Only by a personal choice can life become a total form of a living awe and worship to God(dess). However for those that choose to live in doubt and fear. Will only choose to harvest such darkness from their collective lives. For that is all they see as dear children sulking in the shadows of the living. Be instead of the mindset of the living glories and sacred wonders of life. By being so you will maintain your sense of presence as a "Child of God". In doing so a facet of this "Grand Mystery" of life will reveal itself in harmony with how well you can Love in unconditional terms. Amen.

Children:

Children have one of the greatest gifts of bringing out our Divinity. The innocence of youth teaches us how to care for others and to be mindful of how souls in heaven need not want a harsh reality brought on by a state of lack. The inner Light of children can be so pure and idealistic as to heal the pain of a former generations neglect or hatred. Be open to the glory of God(dess) that shines so bright within children. Do not rebuke their sincerity and curiosity, lest you unwittingly undermine the work of the Angels all around you. For the good willed always promote the best that humanity could ever achieve. Be it by the sweat of your hands, minds, and especially of your combined hearts. Following a single purpose of a shared destiny for yourselves and for your children's children. Amen.

--

If one seeks to be loved the most during the course of a lifetime. It is best to seek out the love of children of all ages out in this world of ours. It is only with the innocent at heart that such a pure love can be displayed in the giving and receiving for the highest grace of all. The love of children in all that is wholesome and true will engender a reality of wonder. That transcends the hardships found in a difficult world.

The children of all manner of species of life are the future promise of their respective heirs. Given this truth we are required in a sacred trust to keep them as pure and alive in spirit as possible. Not because we owe it to ourselves, but because we owe it to God as manifested "Life" itself. This is the gift that crosses generations for the good of all that is holy and beautiful in creation. Amen.

Christians:

As Christians do we choose to celebrate the resurrection of our Savior Jesus Christ or celebrate the crucifixion? Yes, Christ died on the cross for our sins of the flesh. But do we celebrate the death or the life of our savior? Throughout Christendom our faith has been used as a political tool of oppression by Kings and Popes. To subjugate our enemies be they pagan to our ways or worse our own brethren. We crucify them in the spirit of death and not the spirit of reconciliation that our Savior has taught us. Do we need another Savior to come to Earth to die again upon another crucifixion for our sins? The return of our Lord Jesus Christ must first occur in our hearts and minds compassionately. Just as he lived his life righteously and mindfully of the harsh limitations of this world of ours. Before we meet again our Lord and Savior Jesus the Christ to give an accounting of our lives on Earth. We must not be hypocrites of the crimes conducted in the name of God and Christ.

We must forgive but not forget the lessons taught in both blood and tears that Christ shed for us upon his crucifixion so long ago at Calvary. As Christ once said in Matthew verse 25:40 and I paraphrase "What you do unto the least of these, you do unto me".

Clarity:

Truth is truth. It has always existed and will never end. It is only our human awareness that is playing catch up to it. Mostly discovered through unfortunate circumstances and yet also discovered in the sublime moments of clarity.

Clothing:

Clothing of all sorts and colors be they for causal wear, work uniforms, or formal wear are often a facsimile of the auric hues of our very soul. Those who enjoy wearing and designing clothing are remembering on a soul level. The wondrous rays of colors all our spirits enjoyed displaying in creation and inside heaven itself. The multifaceted shapes and patterns of clothing mimic our souls tendency to communicate via patterns of ethereal light and colors. Like many wondrous things in creation, clothing can be a beautiful art form be it in "Au Couture" or in normal daily wear. Amen.

Creating:

Expect the best and you shall find it, expect the worst and likewise you will surely find it in equal proportions. Those are the simple and eternal laws of co-creating with God(dess) our maker. They are total and neutral in absolute forms of expression by intent through ones "Mind's Eye". For either good or bad, both expectations as intentions take the same energy to create what one desires or one incessantly worries about foolishly.

Creation:

We call our oceans a sphere of inner space and on our Earth it is a virtual Garden of Eden to the very depths of the sea floor. I believe the infinite sphere of what we term as outer space beyond our fragile planet. Is a macro representation of our micro inner space of the oceanic ecological system. Consider the Earth or entire Universe as the placenta of God(dess) womb being reborn each moment in a paradoxical manner. What science refers as the "Big Bang" theory is none other the conception as such of an infant being in the bosom of creation.

--

The beauty of God's absolute light is that it is contagious and liberating. With its total truth offered in the form of unconditional love. All who are of the living experience this Holy Light of God from one relative degree to another, whether knowingly or not. Some would state that only humanity can cherish and value God's good graces. I say just look at the splendor of life surrounding you on display by mother nature. Watch as how abundant life is with itself, as plants and flowers blossom. How the very fiber of all that is biological is thriving around you, just like in the tales of the "Garden of Eden". Truth and Love are universal and not tied to any one species. No matter how such a species declares dominion over all others. Life and the natural kingdom will continue unabated whether humanity is here to enjoy the wonders on display or not.

All of life by orders of scale has a soul guaranteed by God himself. Any one soul or spirit isn't superior to the next. All are created equal, because God is an all inclusive god with no favorites. No matter how the Divine reveals itself to mother nature by a sacred matrimony. All forms of worship to God in praise and love are equal throughout this majestic creation. Amen.

--

We are the Ancients as ageless souls created in the Image and Likeness of our Creator God(dess). Brought forth across eternity to this Life once more to live, grow, and die again thus returning back to the creator in spirit. God, first made the Angels as the ageless souls than Eden or the created Universe was given form and this was good. We are the physical living embodiment of those ageless souls or Angels given physical form. Our spirits may lay dormant as we regain our spiritual identity according to the grace of our actions. Otherwise we forget and in the forgetting lose recognition of our inherent Divinity for this life we have been given as a gift.

God, does not create in error. He does create in Infinite forms that may vary by physical appearances, but all share an equal Image of him as embodied souls. We are all heirs to the Kingdom of God, be this kingdom within Eden as the creation or within the ethereal landscapes of heaven and hell. Just as we have been given physical form as mortals paradoxically we have been given spiritual form as immortals in spirit. Immortals in so much as we are those Ancient ageless souls all created before Eden was given form.

As life cycles through by restoration so do the ageless souls cycle through physical lives. Whatever the "Will of God(dess)" may be, we come that we may abundantly fulfill the wisdom of our maker. Not for ourselves alone, but for the good of the many, a good that is all inclusive leaving no one in harm.

Our souls are everlasting just as our father God or mother Goddess is everlasting. In his or her Image we reign within Eden not as conquerors, but as guardians. Live well and Live fully, but do so in consideration of your fellow souls all around you no matter the origin of physical species. For we are all kindred in Heaven. Amen.

--

From our perspective here on earth as mortals we fell from grace in the symbolic chronicle of "Adam & Eve". This is only partly true and the rest of this understanding is skewed by a conditional moralities viewpoint. From the perspective from Heaven there was no falling from grace. Just a transition of one form of living into another. Much like the caterpillar transforms itself into a lovely and gentle butterfly. From the human perspective we are sinners and full of fault tainted by original sin. In the eyes of God we are growing and full of life. We may have transitioned into this world of form. But who is to say that we have actually left the side of God within his throne in Heaven. We are in both places at once as by a miraculous act of his grace be it in Spirit and as incarnated flesh. Due to the indwelling "Spirit of God" within the very fiber and essence of our souls. Amen.

--

What is love? Where does it come from?

Love is the life force of creation. It comes from the dimensions you call heaven. As hate comes from the planes of hell. It is all one meta-reality combined into many sphere's. Much like what you term as of the Earth in your own mortality. Your mortal guise may reside here on this world. But your spirit as well as that of your life resides simultaneously in many realms at once.

As an inkling sliver of God(dess) we all can transverse many realities simultaneously. Since God's Spirit makes it so. We can bring Love from Heaven or we can bring Hate from Hell. It is always our choice in the beginning, middle, and in the end. For it is all one place in this instant moment we call eternity. Amen.

--

Knowledge is only a plump fruit on a tree, it isn't the tree of life itself. If we are soulful explorers, than we are remembering what is already in own hearts for life itself. God(dess) in us and around us, as the fabric of the universe by whatever name we ascribe to his or her own "Holy Spirit".

——

Silence speaks the loudest with its anchored conviction of its sheer majesty of a sublime nature. God's silence dwarfs us all by his holy presence of testament of the glories that are his to offer alone. God's palette of creations continues to leave me dumbfounded and awestruck in its magnitude and variety of orders of life. We are so blessed, yet so conflicted by the incomprehension of it all. Such grandeur of my mere presence leaves me feeling guilty and unworthy to gaze upon such a sublime existence. Yet, I am a part of this orchestra of creation that has become manifested as a form of life unto itself. So than at least by default I am worthy to be here to experience life and its often mundane and extraordinary splendor. Amen.

——

We are the authors, lovers, and dreamers of this creation. What shall we create with our intentions?

I hope as an entity soul that we as a collective overcome this strife we've brought down upon our heads. As an individual entity within the macrocosm of God's Spirit as the maker. Where it is stated, "This to shall pass and fade like the wind". Only unconditional Love can spare us from our self induced madness. That is the grace that God offers all life reborn onto itself. Be still and remember what it is to be Holy once more in the Love of God(dess). Amen.

——

The spark of life what is it?

Is this spark of life a living embodiment of what or whom we term as God? Can this spark of life be both a spark that occurred for an instant and one that stretches the confines of eternity? Perhaps this spark of life had its intent as the very first instance of unconditional love? Where such a love transcends the realms of the physical and the spiritual.

What are we really, are we just God(dess) remembering him or her self for an instant moment?

Creativity:

To be a blessed creator is to have an inborn wonder and awe for life itself. That is best expressed in compassionate qualities for those who shall be the recipients of these kind co-creations with God(dess). Whether these creations be for oneself alone or to be shared abundantly with numerous others in a value like manner. Amen.

Comedy:

Comedians are healers of the heart. Their buoyant comedy transcends the common place into the absurd. Such laughter makes us happy fools in Spirit, but adjusts us to the crazy reality of our day and age. Comedians act as fools, but in disguise they are sharp as a tack. Sages in costume acting like fools but in reality are commentators of our day. A true personification of the "Wise Fool" am I as well. Living, laughing, and crying tears of joy to make peace with this world of ours. Through the grace of God dare I laugh out loud and be heard by my brothers and sisters in Spirit. Amen.

Compassion:

Focus truly on the light of God within ourselves and the Holy Light of God will acknowledge you ever constantly by the gentle hand of grace. By taking you into a sacred blessed place of fulfillment as on an even stride of kindness in all ways. Amen.

--

Humanity by its animal nature versus its spiritual nature is prone to gross inequalities of all sorts. Most evident is how we treat the less fortunate be they economically disadvantaged or physically impaired. We are often more so civilized in name only. To our disgrace we favor opulence over liberty and equality. Thus our human nature will fail us if we do not heed that if the least of us is not represented well in just treatment. It bodes badly for the whole because we are not ready for the mantle of greatness as a humane people much less a nation of civilized people.

Conduct:

What we are as entities of God's light is the "I am" aware of itself but for only an instant. A lover of life expressed in qualitative absolute divine terms that are perfect as made in the image of our creator. However paradoxically flawed as mortal creatures moderated to only achieve excellence in this world of physical senses. In knowing the true beauty of the soul and its potential in the universe of infinity we can govern by the High Holy Spirit within, and not stumble by the selfish whims of an ego based on vanity or worse vice. That is the eternal promise of grace if we shall so seek it out as a living embodiment of the "I am" for this instant once again. Amen.

—–

Those who worship with a hard hand, will also end up with a hard heart. Compassion may be difficult for those who do not yield to a flexible mindset. Only by dealing with others through rigid practices will only lead to a false sense of vindication. Without a flexible hands on approach your personal standards will snap like twigs. Instead of bending with the wind, where discernment and actions will be your guiding truths.

No one person can be perfect, only the "Spirit of God" within us is perfect. As mortal beings we can only strive for excellence due to our frail and vulnerable nature. Be calm when realizing such a personal truth, because being a perfectionist is only a trick of the ego. That will lead you in circles, frustration after frustration. Do not be unforgiving in belief and that only your way is the right way. Having such a self-righteous outlook will lead you to a greater fall back to humility than that which is otherwise warranted. Be gentle but with a firm hand that acts by faith. And, especially by the unconditional love that God can only offer us all by his grace. Amen.

—–

Life is a metaphor of the absolute truth all around us. Those who comprehend its wonder can wield great promise or misery upon others. All depending on their true disposition as a person, whether they be fair and compassionate or selfish and wicked. Only the virtuous person will gain great favor with the "Holy Spirit" in the journey of a lifetime. The deceiver will gain all his promise in the short run if they are cunning. And, if truly despicable in the long run horrors will be committed in order to maintain their perceived authority and power. Both the virtuous and the deceiver will be judged by their actions. Often time the popularity and charisma of the deceiver will over shadow the peoples sense of true justice. Leaving the virtuous person alone from their own fellows and making sacrifices that shall be disrespected by the many.

One person man or woman will gain the world and all its burdens of responsibility. The other man or woman shall gain their own personal dignity and liberty before humanity and God alike. Amen.

Conflict:

When speaking the truth to someone who can not accept it, nor believe you personally. Then such a person is beyond the scope to being reasoned with at all. Not even a neurotic lie will assail them to alter their own personal thinking within that encounter. All they will see and hear is what they wish to within their own warped sensibilities.

It is best to distance yourself from such a disinterested individual if at all possible. Otherwise you may endanger your own peace of mind or the well being of others yet still in your surroundings. Just move along your way without them for the best outcome to be achieved in its entirety.

— —

All those that fight against something will only enhance it through resistance. Instead of fighting to prevail as victorious. One needs to step back away from the ego of perceived separation. To understand that to truly overcome a need one must either support or heal the opposite that is causing the initial conflict. If such a conflict is a circumstance than it is easier to transcend by supporting the competing factors that diminish the perceived wrong. However if a person(s) are the ones that are causing the havoc. One needs to find a compromise to mitigate the distress. If the other group or person is belligerent than abandon them to their own nonsense. And, do your best to resolve a situation without their input or involvement in the matter in question. This is the path to true resolution when dealing with competing factors. Amen.

Consequences:

For those who adamantly state they do not care about the feelings and well being for themselves or that of others. Shall be met with full force by the consequences of there actions to be felt entirely with the salt of pain placed on a wounded heart. By not seeking understanding and consideration in relief of such suffering they are thrust into a vicious loop. Where only mercy and compassion will be the powers that can preserve them from their awful conduct to themselves or others.

Cooperation:

Humanity to date on a global scale often advocates competitiveness as a model of business by a self-righteous indignation. Be it in productivity, logistics, organizational structures, or a plain and simple mindset of niche groups. Akin to how children behave with their favorites, by leaving out those they deem as less than during play. Cooperation outside the business world is deemed more for governments and philanthropic charitable groups whom struggle together to vanquish a common foe. Be it societal ills, or other forms of noble advocacy for humanity or all that is contained within the environment itself.

Yes, every organization and institution has a cooperative mechanism within its whole in order to operate. But, often more than not it will break down into petty inner agency or departmental rivalries to the determent of all. All organizations up to institutions including global corporations need to facilitate a sandbox or "Big Picture" opening. Not just to their own agenda's, but in allowing an opening of a mutual shared agenda with other entities. Not in domination of the other, but to safeguard each one's mission in the world.

Humanity can often devolve in behavior and conduct towards each other that is barbaric versus noble. Natural or man made disasters often bring out this noble inclusive side out of humanity during pivotal points of crisis. Why must humanity wait for a calamity in order to work in its own best all inclusive interest? We can do better, our ideals need not perish together in order to promote superiority over another person(s) or organizational entities. Mimic as best as we can new models of business and social engineering that is one step closer to a heaven and by not acting out in a hell. We need each other, if not now, than certainly later. Humanity thrives more during peace than during conflict, and when we thrive together we all cherish life to a greater whole.

Courage:

The "Sacred Flame" of Life in God's kingdom is one of creation itself. Its aim is to spread the Holy and Divine Light where it is most needed. What is consumes it liberates by grace and not that of discord. It is the function of the Holy Spirit in all matters great and small in Heaven for an eternity. To plan for the righteous "Will of God" to shine brightest where its need is the greatest. Where there is misery there is the "Kingdom of God" acting through his faithful agents for a benediction of the Divine. Do not give up your resolve in the face of an abject fear no matter what the appearances dictate as defeat. Stand fast in spirit if your flesh has become weakened. Allow your heart to lead you if your eyes only see turmoil. And, may your heart be filled with the Spirit of God's unconditional love so that courage will vindicate your resolve in the Lord God. Amen.

--

Seek the unconditional Love of God within yourself and that will be your courage and strength. To live a life fully and well by the graces offered by God and his Angels. Welcome any changes to occur with both patience and tolerance by understanding their purpose to improve your life as whole. Do not condemn yourself with criticisms and judgments that will only divide your resolve and steadfast convictions in the Divine. Be open to the abundant blessings on their way to you as gifts from the "Kingdom of God" in your midst. In stillness you will know the one true God(dess) and how deep an unconditional love can transform you for the better.

Allow yourself to follow the manners and pathway of the righteous. In so doing you will not be led astray but to your own promised purpose in this life that no one can lessen for you. Unfold yourself to all that is worthy of thanksgiving in both humility and wisdom. For in your meekness you shall find the kind handiwork of the Angels all around you. Investing their divinity into you with a compassion that is both heavenly and just. Rest in the fore knowledge that you are not alone and are amongst heavenly relatives of the soul. Protecting, guiding, nourishing, and most of all loving you to be Divine. Amen.

--

Courage is needed when fear needs to be overcome in any circumstance. Bravery is the inner courage that crosses you over an overwhelming predicament into the light of a greater act of good.

D

Death:

I can only Imagine what a soul will encounter upon transcendence of their physical body into the next realm. For those who have experienced near death and speak of a brilliance beyond earthly scope. Perhaps it is being witness to the totality of the one we call God(dess). A Divine Light akin to a celestial star of the Holy Spirit shining and beholding the entirety of creation in one instant. If this is remotely accurate than we have the gift of returning to this moment. Time and again in meditation during our worship of the Alpha and Omega in God(dess). Amen.

--

Our souls are like shooting stars as they pass through this realm we call Life. We have our moments than like all things mortal we lapse back into the life giving arms of our Creator. Much like a child running back into the loving arms of a parent.

Death for mortal beings need not be a tragedy to be horrified about in a cultural mindset. It is but a stage of life we all encounter in our souls progression in eternity. It is not the ultimate ending, it is just a beginning in another form of life to be regarded in a compassionate and sensitive manner. Let go of all cultural conditioning that does harm instead of uplifting the dignity. In all living beings that need to transition to their own promised land of the soul. It is our rightful destiny as incarnated mortal beings returning wholly to our spiritual form in creation. Amen.

Democracy:

In a Democratic nation where the liberties of such a State are severely restricted. It will cease being a democracy and convert either into a fascist or despotic regime. When liberties are suspended during a time of war. It must be treated with total civil transparency by freedom of the press and a government outreach for social justice. Otherwise the Democratic State enters a period of intense jeopardy of its truest identity. The Democratic Nation needs to excel in a governing method of compromise. Otherwise rigid polar extreme stances will lead no where, but to an utter collapse of all social institutions of the land. Delegating them to mere puppets of their former selves where fiat tendencies shall lead to ruin for all.

Desire:

Desires are like flowing water, where one seizes a droplet of water there is always more gushing water to be obtained. So to desire is to be alive. However what one desires must be scrutinized within one's heart. To be of a true need or of a good love for a personal wish fulfillment. Otherwise vanity by ego's lead may yield fulfilled desires that are empty and lack of a true soulful craving. This is the need to be a discerning soul to know what is good and what is bad. Lest you make poor choices that not only harm you, but harm those closest to you in spirit. Amen.

Devotion:

Most of us who have a spiritual inclination that are seeking a greater good in our lives. Must discern how far we are willing to traverse by a holy faith and trust in God's master plan for our personal lives. This is where thought and intent become manifested as our works in faith. We either seek to better our lives and those whom we love dearly through God or we don't. If we do not, we take our chances living our lives with a diminished spiritual capacity and understanding of the Divine. Allowing our spiritual attributes and gifts to hardly be used or worse discovered. Than again if we pick up the mantle as children of a very much alive and dynamic God(dess) in our lives. We can only unleash benevolence by a sheer abundance that will be uncommon to non-believers.

Again depending on your resolve in your faith and personal relationship with God(dess) and the Heavenly host. (Angels, Ascended Masters, Blessed Souls, etc...) It will take years if not decades to a full lifetime to realize how deep your conviction will take you in the Holy and Divine. Many are called by an unconditional Love and temperament to serve this world and the next to come. By service I mean a devotion that is welcomed and not forced upon you. One's permission and good cheer are crucial to embark on such a journey of the evolution of your soul according to the "Will of God(dess)".

Once the journey begins it will stall, stop, and begin anew like a vehicle short on fuel. These are the initial years of the growing pains of shedding your little self and assuming your bigger Self in Spirit. Like an onion you will peel away the layers of misinformed living and the behaviors that no longer serve you as a whole. Once you arrive at the core of your being after perhaps more than a decade. You shall realize that all the knowledge, wisdom, and abilities you had sought were already in your soul. It only took the journey of life for your heart and mind to catch up in knowing. Knowing such a deep truth you shall entertain many angels and souls. That will continue to aid and inform you by a grace that is unlimited through God. The service of the Divine comes in cycles as one is able and willing to walk this infinite path of the soul by an unconditional Love. Amen.

--

Where your interests lay there amongst your pile of favorites is your passion. Those things or activities that motivate you to hopefully act for a good rather than an evil. Such objectives of a devotion always takes us away from our troubles. Albeit it can also lead us astray if we begin to obsess akin to an addictive lifestyle. Where habits yield to patterns that become destructive to yourself and your personal relationships. Only pursue a devotion in moderation and not as a fanatic. This will ensure a steady pace for living your one life right now. Do not allow others of a like mind to deceive you. Otherwise you too will suffer like them when you encounter misery after misery. Keep to the center and devote yourself to what is true and compassionate. This will ensure your peace of mind and be sure to keep good fellows in your company. For they shall be the bedrock that will aid your own personal support in times of need. Do not follow temptations for they will eventually burn holes in your heart and mind. Instead pursue your truest joys filled with a loving passion. That will lead you to your own version of the promised land of the soul. This is the path to a devotion of the most wholesome manner known to all. Amen.

Dharma:

We've been told in our lives to pursue a vocation that interests us with glee and love in our own hearts. This is following the dharma within our souls to marry it with our working career for the well being of our lives. Otherwise we shall lead a fragmented path in our wrongfully chosen career.By mistreating ourselves and others around us with discord and disgust. To a degree that will cause problems to our holistic health be it in physical or soulful bodies via dysfunctional stress. Instead seek out the joy and love in your life where you do not invalidate your passion in dharma. Where peace and happiness will reign both at work and be brought home by living kindly and compassionately to your very own souls worth.

—

When you do a labor of love all your own it is a divine experience to be enjoyed. Such a dharmic passion aids the whole world as God shall be your witness to the joy in your heart and in your work. Do not allow difficulties to disturb you. Just carry on with your love and your love will enfold you and deliver you to your worthy destination. Be careful not to get cocky nor self-centered to the point you lose sight of the reason and intention of your passion. Otherwise you shall invite misery and pain to take you down into an abyss. Be open to making mistakes, but also be open to learning and making corrections as needed. Remember it is such an unconditional love acted upon that shall take you through a joy where wonders will shower you always by grace. Amen.

--

Each person must be their own best servant. According to their own desires where they will rule or be ruled by others due to their own ineffectiveness. In as much as personal choices dictate desirable outcomes as for a fulfilling livelihood. If not such a person will feel confused that why has life taken a turn for the worst. Why are they always receiving or causing unwanted stress factors in their personal life. Such uncertainty can easily lead to misery if one does not plan sufficiently to overcome life's barriers. The undisciplined must show courage and move towards a path of redemption. Only than one will begin to gain confidence that they aren't a victim, but a co-creator with God of their own fate. Moving forward stride after stride as the years go by not feeling worse but better for having lived. Living a righteous life no matter how you define it will gain you the favor of the "Holy Spirit". Offering you resources both known and unknown to you to not just merely exist as a survivor. But to thrive by following truly what you love doing. This is the path to paradise found on Earth by a mutual Love with God and your joys. Amen.

--

Those who can marry their work with their joyful past time are being truest to themselves. By allowing grace and good fortune to flood into their livelihood. This is the path of the wise and creative person who can spin wool into gold of the soul. It is the passion of the heart come alive in deed. A passion as a vocation that is not tied to anyone person. By means of a sanctified service from the heart and mind. Amen.

--

For those who know in reincarnation suspect rightly so they can follow their inner obligation. For this life or cast it away like trash to be forgotten. Those that choose by benevolence to follow their inner dharma will not be dismayed, nor will they suffer hardships that are cruel. Those who are acting upon their obligation by sacred purpose for this life. Will be honored in return by writing upon their hearts and minds their purpose by grace. It is always a willing companion to unite one's purpose with their truest Love.

By an unconditional Love with a sacred intention that can not be forsaken in one's Divine mission for each lifetime. It is a marriage of hearts and minds all focused on the singularity of ultimate creation. To beget more natural and uplifting well being for all concerned. Be well and know your wishes and desires will be purified with the absolute love of God(dess). In a remarkable display of glory for all that is good and holy. Amen.

Dignity:

What is the hallmark of a dignified spirit? It is carrying out the precepts of a silent and humble conduct. That one is not grand standing in order to receive praise or adoration from the vanity of others. So as to enact a sense of confirmation of being valued. One is independent from such leanings and also bind yourself to the lovely nature of a modest conduct. Amen.

Direction:

There are three directions a person can take in their lifetime. The first is the most easiest form of being acted upon without having any sort of plan. Being tossed about life as if your in a stormy ocean wave out in the sea of apathy.

The second is the most seductive form of direction following one's Vices instead of one's heart. Following such a dark path is akin to a direct causeway into the bowels of a living Hell.

The third is the greatest and also the hardest of the three directions in a lifetime. It is following one's heart by joy and sacrifice in an eternal journey of discovery and healing. Healing one's self and most importantly others along this sacred path of Virtue. If one is to picture such a pathway of Light it is a spiraled corkscrew in a direction of ascendency.

Life is a maze of wonders and perils that must be navigated with great care. With God as our witness guided by his Holy Spirit we will always transcend by faith, hope, and love this difficult life of ours.

That is the loving will of God that our lives may be abundant and enriched for having gone this way in Creation. Amen.

Disappointment:

Our disappointments may be many due to numerous reasons of the mind and heart. As we continue to live as people we grow past many of them hopefully for our own good. For those disappointments that are heaviest we must learn how to forgive and surrender them for our highest good to appear. Only then can we release feelings of guilt over time and enter into a fuller experience of what it means to be a fulfilled person. Amen.

Distinction:

To accept and approve of one's character is not the same act. When accepting a person or an event that has transpired one must have the benefit of the doubt. When one approves of a persons conduct or actions one is then supporting such a person or circumstance by one's own filters of judgment. There is clearly a distinction between acceptance and approval of ones conduct or of there actions. Knowing this one can move forward in either supporting such a person or circumstance until such time it it no longer warranted.

Divine Light:

We are but a reflection in the mirror of the Almighty Creator of Life. When we gaze upon the brilliance of the purely Divine light within ourselves. We reveal our truest hidden nature of grace, which is God's immorality within our living beings upon this reality. Amen.

—–

Our inner light within our souls is from the torch of God(dess) as an eternal brilliance. This majestic light is the spark of creation from the very beginning. That still illuminates within us to this very moment. The eternal is pleased with this unceasing resource within the totality of Life. "No One", has a monopoly on this Light! Speakers of the light will come and go much like an unending carousel. However the light of "Truth and Love" is absolute and will continue. No matter what universe you find yourself within as an entity. Amen.

—–

We are the "Light of God" the Majestic. This divine light is the lifeblood of all creation from its simplest to most complex form of being. We must by grace "Shine" truly so as to spread this glorious light of God(dess) within us all. In doing so we set each other free with a diversity that is only mirrored by the beautiful array of all that mother nature herself can offer creation. If we allow this spiritual light within us to be hidden. We are committing an injustice not only to ourselves, but to all who are near and far from our reach.

This "Light of God" is abundant and without limit in its scope and supply. When we give of the "Light of God(dess)" within us. We act as co-creators by shining brightly and purely with an unconditional love. Our "Light" is alive and vibrant as a living praise to the "Glory of God(dess)". Amen.

Divine Order:

Where there is symmetry there is beauty. Whether it be of one order or another of scale. Its harmony transcends limitations imposed on it by others. Who lack a full comprehension of its subtleties and graces. The function of a system full of symmetry does not distinguish between friend or foe. Since both are one and inclusive to the other in the grand scale of life. Amen.

Divinity:

As individuals or what I shall term as "I" energy that is governed by the shifting sights of appearance that often than not are mistaken in regards to circumstance. This none other is truly selfish "ego" energy expressed in disregard of compassion. Then there is the dynamo energy that runs silently and deeply within all Life. This energy I shall term as "We" energy in a united expression that is the benevolent side to God, that I shall focus on. This "We" energy looks not at appearances nor circumstance with eyes from without to within. But only with the very peering focus of truth with unconditional clarity as one utter expression of absolute love, which to the core of being there are infinite expressions to love by.

Since the God of absolute love can not be explained merely in one statement. The flip side however is God can be explained with a very simple mutual tender kiss of true love akin to unleashing the rapture of the heart and mind. Of the holiest of divine senses that our entity engenders is that of God(dess) being our ever constant silent witness but ever active participant. Amen.

—

Child, we as the "Holy Spirit" have never left the side of the one we call "God". Like yourself you have never in Spirit left behind the light of God's bounty on this Earth. Both Spirit and flesh coexist in the same realm we call Heaven. Only in the mind of humanity there is a separation or a flawed distinction called sin. Sin is not blasphemy, it is a mindset prone to error and confusion.

Humanity as a species needs to evolve beyond its own ego prone mindset unto sin itself. Only then humanity can see into the unity of all life, be it in spirit or flesh. Draw upon your spirit and usher forth unconditional love so as to ease this unneeded pain of a mind based on sin. This is the true Atonement of evolution as a being of Divinity. As all of life truly is meant to be created according to the "Will of God". Amen.

—–

Our beloved Creator gave breath to all that was, is, and will be again. In doing so with such an unconditional and total intent of love. That all other hardships of mortality cease to be the case. Our maker of all that is life imbued with the very essence as both the living creator and the created being. In one full loop of the circle of life the "Holy Spirit" permeates totality. Never far away but always beyond cursory recognition of a mortals perception. What is not seen, is than felt as an ever evolving relationship with all that is. An Infinite bond that can not be undone nor forgotten amongst a dynamically living link with all creations of the Beloved. Amen.

—–

Our souls are immaculate due to the indwelling "Spirit of God" within our being. Such a state of inner grace is wonderful to behold in the scope of a sweet tenderness that a person can achieve in this life. However with a perfect soul we are full of contradictions due to the human condition. Humanity much like any physical beings in mortality are flawed by their own essential nature. Thus the inner striving for a higher truth in living is made that more elegant in the eyes of creation. We are God(dess) in the Infinite variety of life as mother nature so vividly displays in a sublime array of abundance.

Who are we to deny this truth and yet condemn each other or worse ourselves with illusions. Surrender yourself to your inner Immaculate soul and truly live in a dynamic Miracle we call everlasting Life. Amen.

Dream:

Idle dreams are like vagabond fools going from place to place and returning home. If a conscious dream lacks substance then it to will more than fade away like dust in the wind. Sub-conscious dreams are of another matter of well being that speaks to your overall spirit within. Their symbolic language is best understood by subtle traits that are mostly personal to the dreamer. Otherwise generalized dream reference materials become an unruly misfit in interpreting your personal sub-conscious dream sleep states. Shallow day dreams are another matter under heaven for they are portals to what your desiring the most. Sometimes what you desire the most is wrong for you. Other times it is more right for you than you can realize. It is only you are not prepared or sufficiently ready to seize your dream in reality.

Thus if you dream or day dream too deeply you shall suffer from want. Making yourself a slave to your desires no matter if they are good or ill for you. Be wary of your desires that become an obsession for they may only end up badly if you lose your perspective. Keep still and stay centered in the truth and not only your version of the truth. Stay alert and self aware for your dream may become a reality only in partnership with the Divine. Amen.

Dreaming:

When one dreams during sleep whether or not these dreams are remembered and what they represent by their very nature. We are all taping into the Great Spirit of God by ease dropping on the total experiences of creation. Dreams yes can be fanciful, symbolic, or prophetic but yet they are also a living embodiment of what is occurring in a fluid state of ethereal motion. Both the dream state of rest and the living awakened presence of living are both simultaneously the same environ. The only difference in perception is one is experienced as a human being and the other as a spiritual being.

Dreams:

Dreams are like a personal mirror using our own internal language on the theater of your Imagination. It is all a personal reflection of your most inner self acting out what it needs to express and share to you personally. Dreams are your best inner guide to what troubles you or what fascinates you. Dreams are also the portals to inspiration and prediction in one's life. Listen well to your dreams via your minds eye. Since your highest self is telling you something of value and grand importance. Amen.

Duty:

Whatever one does with a heartfelt purpose it will be treated in Heaven and on Earth as holy in the eyes of God. Such a heart moving purpose includes joy, passion, and love all showcased by your duties. Where such attributes that exist in the activity itself also simultaneously shine brightest within God whom is always in your midst. Since these very qualities are amongst the forces God employs to convey his "Holy Will" in creation. Forget not these precepts of service in what functions you hold as a sacred activity. Where you to will be truly blessed by duty and providence. Amen.

E

Ego:

The ego can be considered humanities greatest folly known to us. The splintered ego has caused so much unjust separation that it can bring discomfort just to consider. Where if we fathomed its total implications for the self and society at large. We would be dumb struck by the inadequacies caused by the many and the few. How selfish behaviors either by misconduct or pursuit of an ideology in order to sabotage another point of view or way of life. Can cause so much pain that only idiots would relish in sharing to the degree that it has existed among a society as a whole.

However one thing is for certain that the ego is a biological construct, meaning a behavioral form of adaptation to our environment. It is only through this awareness can we dip into the aspect of the soul as its counter-balance. The soul or "Spirit of God(dess)" within all life, redeems us from our follies and faults. When humanity reaches a stage of evolutionary development that the soul has as much bearing in our actions than the mortal flesh. Then the scales of our divinity would tip in our favor individually and combined as a civilization. Until that time in our future or our children's future we make do with the just and unjust all around us. Amen.

--

Empowerment:

One of the gifts of being resourceful is giving yourself permission to be self-empowered for your own welfare, and that of others.

Endurance:

We are all on God's time table although we often conclude otherwise. How we create and follow through on our self made daily routines is an illusion of control. Those with an open mind may be more flexible in accepting this fact. All the rest will still struggle and bemoan ironically why God should allow "such and such" to occur. If only such persons would be willing to remove the shudders upon their mind's and hearts. Will they see it is not so much what has happened to us or those we dearly love. But how we pick ourselves up and carry on in a dignity that is intent on a progressive inner growth back to God's love.

Life will be filled constantly with peak's and valley's. How we prepare our heart's and mind's to make such crossings will reveal our true grit to live fully and well. Begin to amass the spiritual and life long tools that will assist you according to your own personal circumstances. Allowing the proper fore knowledge, wisdom, and hope to carry you onward in a authentic confidence that will be long lasting. Even in the clutches of fears and doubts you will surmount your troubles.

Your focus on goodness will help define your total life. By not permitting one bump on the road to break the wheels of your destiny. God through your being will stand up for you. As long as you maintain and live your truth which is in his love for you. The grace of God will trickle in at first until at one much needed point in your life it will drown your troubles like a flood that will know no end. Amen.

Enlightenment:

Every "Ah-Ha" moment is like a beacon of truth shining for an instant in your mind's eye. This is the gift of clarity experienced by the receiver whom is usually often more than not glad to have been exposed to it entirely. Such is the path to self-discovery filled with awe to have become aware of what is required and needed in most cases. Welcoming such experiences allows us the receiver to become illumined in such a manner that understanding will unfold time and again. Where wisdom and especially fore knowledge becomes acceptable by its own sublime nature of such an enlightened time spent in meditation or contemplation. Making a space for an ethereal place will allow wonders to enter in where only before ignorance stood upon your mind.

Be calm and be curious enough to spark your imagination in order to allow questions and associations in thought to take hold. If not briefly, than for moments at a time until the spark of truth deepens in your own being. This is the way to unfolding your own divinity by way of worship and communion with all that is holy and good. Amen.

--

When praying all we need do is offer an unconditional love to God(dess) and seek to be filled by his / her own "Holy Spirit". In doing so we need not ask for things of this world. Be they materialistic nor alterations to our circumstances in this current life we have right now. Yes, this is contrary to all we have been taught in order to worship our God(dess) who art in paradise. This is the path less traveled for those that still need to be cared for and be provided for in order to live a good life. When seeking to be filled with the "Holy Spirit" or the totality of God's abundance that is his nature to give freely. We need to be receptive as living vessels to such a blessing by surrendering our human needs and wants. To him who cares more for us than we can fathom through our mortal comprehension.

As we surrender akin to a discipline of mindfulness we open ourselves up to the wonder and glory of the "Kingdom of God" all around us. Where at first the path is difficult, but worthy of those who are truly faithful and filled with a compassionate conviction not of this world. The first blessings will be small, but once your dedication grows through the years. So do the miracles you get to glimpse all around you and in the acts of the "Holy Spirit" upon others. Providence and grace take hold of you and squeeze you like a love no one person could ever give you. Trust in the process, no matter if doubts and the lack of understanding of others try to dissuade you of your course of action. Be filled with a sense of gratitude and awe of what the mystery of life is teaching you. As you continue to grow as a person and a Divine soul those with an open heart will be the first to take notice of your good and just deeds.

By continuing such a discipline you will become a fountain of life, light, and most of all an unconditional love. That will nourish you to the point you will have achieved the goal of being filled truly with the "Holy Spirit". Sought so long ago by your innocent former self not fulling realizing the path to be undertaken. But that courageous person long ago has made you who you are now and shall continue to become by grace. Amen.

--

How do I find enlightenment? One doesn't find enlightenment, it finds you by grace. One does not earn enlightenment, one fulfills it much as one fulfills honesty. It is all a matter of practice and not a matter of receiving. It is peace in action and not peace by inaction. It is the way to reconciliation of our mortality with our spirituality. It is life in abundance versus life in misery. It is a kinship with others versus isolation from existence. It is being one with creation, instead of acting separate from reality. We are enlightened when we live on purpose with "Love & Truth" as our service to Life. Amen.

Eternity:

A secret place in time is what is termed as eternity. It is a living phase of existence often overlooked by mere mortal activities. Its impacts are varied from a raised consciousness due to the inter-connectivity of all life. Or the transition of events that are not in a neat Modus Operandi. Eternity as a force is not one of conformity, but of action guided by the orchestration of life. It is a vast ocean of movement that on the surface is misunderstood. But at its depths performs paradoxically like a ballet.

--

"Precept of Time & Eternity"

In a moment one can understand eternity. As a concept of no time at all. Eternity is but an instant, one moment in time but paradoxically it consists of no time at all. This instant for eternity to a mortal is incomprehensible due to a linear view point. From the point of view of eternity it is a fully non-linear as one whole moment. A linear time scale is set at the slowest time dilation for mortal perception of creation. For eternity which consists for an instant, it is set at full velocity ahead. Or full momentum without any restrictive dilation's of time. To understand a mundane moment is to understand all of creation in but an instant of time itself. Amen.

--

For what we term as an instant is but a blink of the eye, a moment and none other. For God(dess) an instant is what we call "Eternity" a Holy Divine instant. A flash of life in the mind of God. Eternity is a timeless moment all but known as an instant that is a drawn out stretch of time for mere mortals. But a non barrier for Spirit to transcend "Heaven and Earth" in this space we call creation. Amen.

--

Eternity is but one instant moment we call by the phenomena we know as time. This one instant moment is a stasis field in a transfixed position, frozen but yet dynamic in motion. A living paradox, but yet not so. Eternity is one instant moment where God is in a trance with us as abiding with his creation. Constantly being remembered and forgotten over and over again. Creating infinite parallel realities to recreate in a grand living thought of a living reflection of his being. Eternity is not a place but a state of mind as an extension of the affect of God engaging in thought. Amen.

Evangelism:

Those that attempt to evangelize through coercion will only lead astray the followers. True conversion to an ideology be it secular or religious must come from within the stirring of one's inner soul. Otherwise false testimony will ensue out of political convenience than a professed truth of one's own heart.

If true conviction is to be found in worship it must be proven in acts of earnest behavior. Or else one will be shallow to him or herself much less those that will depend on you in your personal interactions. True faith must be formed from within one's own authority of the Spirit of God within them. Otherwise you'll become ripe to be exploited and manipulated by those with wicked intentions. Whether they speak the name of God or not. There time will come and it will come at full strength unless repentance is so desired, asking for mercy or forgiveness. Of those that convert others insincerely to a belief or professed faith that lie in their hearts of hearts. Amen.

Evil:

There is no honor in darkness, no Light of truth exists. Be weary of seeking promises of favor from any form of evil. Unless you seek your guaranteed demise at every turn of opportunity. There is no loyalty amongst evil doers, only the chance to succeed or be squashed by an ill tempered person. Be mindful of whom you associate with, or you'll be in pain more often than actually being very well off. Stay clear of mockery and trickery that leads to the misfortune of others. Or your turn will come sooner than later to being mocked and becoming an unfortunate person. It is often better to take an indirect path in life where hardship is a given in regards to moral behavior. Than to take the easy street and rewards up front by cheating yourself down the line. Whoa to the fool who cares not for reason or wisdom. You are already dammed by your own inequities and will need more than twice the effort in recovering your dignity.

F

Faith:

As Jesus the Christ said in Matthew 17:20 to have faith the size of a mustard seed to move mountains. Well these mountains aren't of the Earth, more likely they are the personal mountains of a person's spirit. That needs adjusting for the sake of righteous betterment on an holistic level. Thus the path of faith will lead us to being remade in the Holy Light of God(dess). For our mutual grace forever more in a steadfast manner in this realm we call Life.

--

The beauty of God's inner light within us all is that it shines the blessed truth upon our lives. By always displaying the compassionate truth in a Spirit of Joy. Where our thanksgiving enriches the experience for us and that of God's joy in us. Our faithfulness must be based in both truth and that of love. A love that is both forgiving and life giving in nature. Otherwise we succumb to pettiness in attitude and conduct towards each other in spirit and actions. Be open to receiving the first fruits of the season from the Holy Spirit. In receiving grace from God we become stewards in return to share such a grace to our brothers and sisters in Spirit. Be mindful of your pledge to God and God will act so richly as to overwhelm your senses by an absolute love. Amen.

--

Those who have questioned God's existence by stating where is he? Can be assured that God can not be seen by mortal eyes, but by faith alone. Only with spiritual senses can one see, smell, taste, touch within, and hear their creators being in all of our lives sensibly. The very act of sensing God(dess) in our midst invites the sacred to unfold for those who are earnest in spirit of the most Divine of all in creation. Listen to the spaces in between spaces, the thoughts between thoughts, and there you shall find the witness observing the observer. Amen.

––

Our faith when coupled with unceasing gratitude will open one's attitude. To one of wholeness and prosperous thinking by living such a fine lifestyle. It is a path of awakening to your own spirit within and its abundant treasures from the vault of God's bosom. Be still and know when one maintains a harmony of Spirit. One's attitude can surmount obstacle after obstacle. Have faith in yourself and your creator with full thanksgiving. Amen.

––

We know of miracles we that are faithful to God, but we forget constantly. Treating them as if they never happened whereby skeptics demand proof of this or that. Cynics will never be placated to with their closed stances and posturing. Their bias is already set firmly into their foundation of preconceived notions. Cynics should not be ignored lest they become entrenched in their ideology in regard to doing harm to spiritual believers. Neither should cynics be embraced as equals for they lack faith. Although they can love just as we do to the fact that they are ever evolving much like ourselves in comprehension.

Yet the path of their own choosing is made by free will in order to understand the greater reality at large. Miracles are for all be they religious or secular in mindset guarded by a righteous conduct lived in moderation. Those of a restricted mindset are susceptible to half-truths and plain lies living at times as zealots in an extremist fashion. Miracles are independent to any of the ideologies of whom they are revealed to as a gift from the divine. Those who are faithful full of gratitude will always be receptive to the majestic authority of God. All others will suffer from an emptiness that knows no bounds be it in spirit or purpose. For they know not the glory of God that resides in their very own souls. Amen.

Final Judgment:

The "Final Judgement" for each soul that has ever lived be it sentient or not. Is not a judgement, rather a review that is done in familiar surroundings with souls you shall deem as loving and wise. To show the soul entity how all of life is intertwined beyond the petty responses of the ego or the illusion of the mind fostering separation. All thoughts, intentions, and acts of that very spirit in a lifetime will be shared in order not to persecute, but to liberate the soul of their Earthly identity. To nurture a sense of collective belonging to God(dess) and all that has ever been and shall be again by the "Will of God". To show that soul what and how the tenderness of God(dess)'s love has enfolded them. Throughout a lifetime, whether they were aware of it and especially when they were not.

How many servants of the Lord God came as spirits, Angels, and people to your aid within a lifetime and how you welcomed them or how you dismissed them. Where the sense of fear in your minds and hearts was false and more often than not never materialized. This "Final Judgement" will also advocate as a witness how deeply you loved in caring for yourself and especially for others. Where compassion was offered and how it was distributed out through family, friends, and strangers alike.

We are all Holy divine beings made in the Image and likeness of God(dess) our creator. So the "Final Judgement" will review how God(dess) (him or herself) lived through us as a form of holy gratitude for having come this way once more in creation. Amen.

--

For those events in a lifetime that happen to us that we do not fully comprehend their meaning. Is to accept the mystery we call life and to know when our term comes to cross over into our true spiritual form through the "Spirit of God". Then we can be shown what has transpired in its fullness from the eyes of the "Host of God". To be revealed the wonders and missteps in our personal lives. So we may gain a fuller comprehension in order to value all forms of interactions with each other and those forces that are beyond us. This is but one example of the proverbial "Final Judgement" we all encounter as we return from the realms of mortality into our ageless spiritual bodies. Amen.

First Contact:

All of life in creation according to their order of being exist. With the very same attributes we term as the essence of humanity. Humanity does not hold any exclusivity to such characteristics of being in both spirit and in conduct. The truest foundation stems from the oversoul of all Life. Which we often refer to as God(dess) the omnipotent deity. The "God of Gods" has his essence in all sentient life across all creations. We are but one example of his majesty amongst the stars. We will encounter others yet still foreign to our ways, but not a foreign spirit of God indwelling their souls. Before we condemn them for their differences out of a sense of fear of the unknown. We must first listen to our common Divine soul within all of us. What does it sincerely say to you? Is war preferably to peace, is genocide better than inter-marriage?

Are cultural and religious exchanges destructive or do they actually display our similarities in God's Spirit? Be mindful what is preservation of our species under the argument of purity. Recalling our pure history as both war mongers and that of renowned artists and engineers. Otherwise the ones to fear the most will not be them who are God's children from another world, but that of ourselves. Becoming the abhorrent Devils we wish to be cleansed of in totality.

Free Will:

Paradise is what you make of it, whether one wants "Hell or Heaven on Earth". It shall be, that indeed is a very generous God(dess) to allow his creations to ruin themselves by free choice. If necessary for the sake of maturing as souls in eternity.

--

Humanity and any other sentient life out in the cosmos is a living paradox much like us. We are equally capable of atrocities guided by the selfish whim of free will. Yet so are we also capable of brilliant acts of good will towards each other. It is all based on the disposition of the being guided by their inner sense of wonder or travesty.

--

What we call free will is a tremendous gift from God. This gift is but a chance to fulfill our role in life for the highest good of all. Or we can ruin this gift by wasting ourselves and our environment around us into oblivion. However a God(dess) of absolute Love will always redeem us with the benefit of a grace that is everlasting. Do we exercise this gift of "Free Will" with prudence or do we waste it by our own personal misgivings for each passing moment? That is our gift to decide the outcome. For those that witness free will and its consequences by the atrocities of mankind. Have watched how humanity has chosen poorly and is laying waste to the "Garden of Eden". Be mindful of this powerful gift of free will and thus be good stewards of such a grace. That is when it is rightly used for the betterment of all. Amen.

Fools:

If one is speaking to a foolish person, than the foolish person will only hear nonsense. Since a fool can not understand truth when it is conveyed by reason. Such a foolish person will only understand their own warped mentality. Communication will always be impaired through their own restrictive perception. No matter if truth dances before them in its fullest glory. The only bridge in order to communicate with a foolish person if so desired. Is to locate a common interest and gauge similarities where parallels can be drawn out in order to convey your point of view to them. Where for a brief moment in time a comprehension can be shared for whatever gains can be made to a degree.

Forgiveness:

Forgiveness is a gift and a tool of the healer from within. The balm of forgiveness is meant to soothe first the one who is earnestly pursuing such an inner gift. Whatever else that remains than goes to the offender silently in peace. Without alerting the other person(s) that such a grace has been extended to them at all. This is the way of anonymously healing oneself in solitude during the process of application of this grace. One will not ever run empty on the supply of the gift of forgiveness. For it springs forth from the fountain of God's abundant love for all his creations. Allowing forgiveness as a practice in recovering our peace mind is not only a gift to oneself and the intended recipient, but also back to God. Letting him know you care enough for your brothers and sisters in Spirit as you care for yourself. Honor the sacred gift of forgiveness and it will alleviate your pain and set you free by God's absolute love. Amen.

--

There is an ancient truth that has been seldom remembered across the ages of creation. This truth is one of release from any evil in one's life by circumstance or curse. It is to forgive with a great unconditional open heart by love. Be it your plight or the issuer of a wicked curse. Such a forgiveness of compassion invites the God of life, light, and love into the situation. By steadfast conviction to such a brave resolution of forgiveness. Opens up the heart of true benevolence for mercy and grace to pour forth without end. Amen.

--

It is a gift from God our maker that we have the ability to forgive ourselves and others. But truly forgiveness needs to be unconditional. If not conditional forgiveness tied to demands is completely false. Much as is conditional love tied to limits imposed on another or upon yourself. Love and forgiveness are gifts from God that flow unconditionally and should be shared as such. Amen.

--

I can only forgive another or myself with unconditional love that is unceasing. Otherwise I fail upon my intent to heal myself or the situation at hand. I must stand firm upon the rock of faith if I am to transcend a transgression done to myself or another. For this is the path of reconciliation for my own sake and that of my brothers and sisters in spirit. A spirit that is not my own for our spirit in God is shared in oneness by grace. No one can separate my spirit from another for to attempt such an act is impossible. We are tied to each other spiritually for either better or worse. Let us than proceed in harmony not just for our own sakes but in a spirit of thanksgiving within God. Amen.

--

Those who state that "Time heals all wounds" have forgotten one very important rule. That forgiveness must first occur for the internal healing of the emotional wound. Otherwise the grief or anger will fester within one's self like a cancerous tumor. Forgive those whom that have harmed you, and especially one's self for harming others. Than and only then can time begin to heal the wounds of the heart once more. Amen.

--

To love unconditional is to be able to forgive unconditionally. For without the capacity to love, one will lack the capacity to forgive in return. Both love and forgiveness are agents of Divine change that overcome all adversity. By turning adversity on its head and making it into a sublime gift of strength and providence. So love unconditionally where you will then have the capacity to forgive unconditionally. Otherwise slights, grudges, pains, and betrayals will not heal without forgiveness in the fullness of time. Amen.

--

Forgiveness is medicine for the heart of the giver and receiver. If there is no receiver to be had than the "Holy Spirit of God" shall stand in there place. To help comfort and aid the giver of forgiveness. Forgiveness is an elixir of life allowing slurs, hates, and other maladies of the heart to be released. So as to nourish with love a person's spirit allowing them to return to wholeness in mind, heart, and body. Forgiveness brings harmony and balance as a form of spiritual atonement. It shall benefit more the giver of forgiveness than the receiver, for that is its intended purpose. So as to soothe a splintered ego. Amen.

Fulfillment:

If one is to live an abundant life. One must seek out all manner of ways to be challenged. Otherwise the fountain of the flow of life will only trickle in. One needs to perturb the flow of life so as to engage it fully. Rich engagement is the fruit of enlightened labor of one's passion by a sense of fulfillment.

G

Gamers:

Those that revel in electronic games do so with a zeal. For gamers express themselves in so many profound and subtle terms. Much like an artist depicting a scene before us to enjoy and be captivated by in its fullest splendor. Gamers are learning all the time, but it is by choice if they choose to mature via play. They have fun like children, but do so with value of the many relationships created through a kinship of play. Each gamer defines their own joy with themselves and with new and old friendships alike all in its proper emphasis. The games are the mediums to self expression and self discovery of who they wish to be and who they are by their very own nature.

--

Generosity:

Thank you God that we can give and be blessed for the giving in the very same instance. By a selfless love we know this truth that by giving we all share with a spirit of Joy and Thanksgiving. For God(dess) has given us his/her own bounty to use as we see fit. Hopefully we follow in the foot steps of the saintly by their guidelines of benevolence. Lest we use God's bounty within creation as not a gift, but as weapon to separate each other from our own good. Lo to the fool(s) that choose such a path for they shall reap miseries upon their heads. That only repentance in a true spirit of reconciliation can ever console back to wholeness. Amen.

Genius:

When a prodigy or a genius of one sort or another on this Earth is discovered. It is assumed they are a self-contained wonder and phenomena of our universe. They are however as much as an evolved soul reborn into our world to a life seeking atonement.

Their innate abilities are from the wellspring of their eternal spirit more so easily harnessed and utilized readily. By doing so they are very tactile in nature having what to others appears to be an accelerated learning capacity. To them it is a common non-chalet experience more mundane than extraordinary. There on lookers reactions are often surreal or childlike exuberance of how their gifted genius exceeds rational.

Some of these geniuses with a faulty mindset based on ego are mostly looking for a worthy challenge. By relieving their boredom for an activity or a challenger as they see fit to fill a vacuum within their being. Nonetheless these challenges are usually often than not short lived aberrations that come and go. The genius mindset needs to be wary of singularly seeking only as a form of lust a remarkable challenge. Where obsessions can become rooted and lead to an eventual schism from reality and a self induced social isolation.

The way out of this vicious loop ushered by one's ego is that of humility by proactively seeking to be of service to others. By a conduct of moderation such a genius will eventually find a purpose to wrap their gifts around.

Such a genius will have untold experiences of meaningful exchanges with others for the highest good of many. Especially with life itself thus aiding their genius to further develop in a wholesome manner of growth.

The hallmark of a genius is not to know everything or to be a specialist in their field of expertise. But how can they have the greatest beneficial impact to those they can help with their inner passions.

––

Genius without conflict is idiocy manifested. Even geniuses need to be tempered hard like steel to stand the test of the ages. For a genius without a challenge is a fool waiting to self destruct from boredom. A genius without a purpose is a travesty and a deliberate loss upon the greater fabric of society. Where the loss of any genius whether (s)he be discovered or not is a near crime onto itself. A masterpiece on display without an audience to enjoy the wonders and marvels to be created is a pity. Forget not your role in life with those genius's with a sense of humility. For without a purpose you are not just lost to us, but from yourself as well.

Grace:

Where it has been stated that absolute power, corrupts absolutely. Then what is one to seek in its place for self governance amongst guiding others unto a specified mission? It is none other than absolute "Grace", which is the purified form of power. Where power by nature can corrupt too easily but grace is perfectly suited to transform the lives of oneself and that of others. Without causing harm in the pursuit of it nor reflect poorly unto oneself in achieving a place of ease and stability. Grace is a derivative of Love, where power is kin to Lust.

Grace is smooth, balanced, sorted and filtered that it can uplift a soul beyond the clutches of the world. By seeking "Grace" in unconditional manners although in moderation life will once again be full of awe even in common experiences. Amen.

――

From our routine lives that often feels forced upon us as a life of existence. By faith can only become meaningful when we invite the sacred Spirit of God into our personal lives. Such an invitation can bring a change of pace that borders on a blessed surreal mix of events. That shares grace with yourself, and among those who are close to you in your life. God's bounty does not ever discriminate towards those who seek his Holy Will of absolute Love.

――

Where grace is a simple blessing from God(dess). A selfish hunger for Power can become a complex burden to carry for those with depraved intentions. Grace is always the path to righteousness. Since it leads to the heart and love of God(dess) as the greatest destination for all souls. Grace can always make destructive power come undone in its entirety for the good of all concerned. Amen.

――

Grace is an expression of a love that is unconditional. Such a love is not timid, nor is it foolish, it is a love that has upheld nations by a common trust. It is the love that both saints and lovers live by to the fullest of delights. Grace when it is released into our shallow experiences it breathes new life into our hearts and minds. This life is one of renewal from the old ways that led us astray. Down alleys filled with shadows and shallow experiences that at times was beneath our fullest expression as people and especially as souls. Grace is the long arm of the Lord God as an agent of the Holy Spirit to carry out the "Will of God(dess)". By allowing grace to take hold in our lives we permit justice and truth of the holiest of spirits to rescue us from ourselves and from this crazy world. Take comfort in such a place and this will become your salvation through the Lord God forever and ever. Amen.

--

When you bless one soul, you will bless them all. Since we are all one meta-entity in Spirit by this realm and in many other forms of existence. We are one akin to a web of conduits to each other. One can not be effected well without affecting all those in their realm of influence. A blessing, an omen, a cheerful toast, saying grace, and a miracle are all methods to reveal ones holy divine identity in this life. Amen.

--

Gratitude and Hope go hand in hand as Sisters where each values what is presented. Gratitude allows for the thanksgiving for what is "Now" and for what has been given. Hope allows for a future form of gratitude to be expressed and perhaps shared with many more souls. Gratitude and Hope are both wonders of the heart that continue to give long after they have occurred. Amen.

Great Mystery:

To those who seek the meaning of life with all its wonders and secrets. The seeking isn't in the destination nor in the journey. It is truly in the meaning it is prescribed to in one's own heart. If one truly sought the totality that life is, than one is seeking God in his infinite outlets. The intention of the sacred is what will bind you to awakening the Divine within. Thus the "Book of Life" will no longer read as gibberish to one who is devout filled with the "Spirit of God". Amen.

Greatness:

If a great (wo)man has no humility than they're a fool in relation to all others. If such a prestigious person lacks the sensibility of having foresight in terms of good conduct by serving with respect. Than (s)he will lack the personal dignity to truly care for others in a fashion that would equate to a true sense of honor. Steer clear of such people, one day their pride will cause them great harm and especially those closest to them. Be wary of the rising super star with selfishness in their hearts of hearts. As quick as they rise to stardom shall they crash back to Earth with a thud to be seen and heard by all. The truly great men or women are great not so much because of their actions, but of whom they are in a form of virtuous living. Amen.

Groups:

Besides the proverbial saying of "Strength within numbers". There is also near perfection when so many differing souls join as one in their combined creative pursuits. Unlike homogeneous and unoriginal uniformity in the world of the mundane. When mortals combine themselves to a fluid and organic group.

There is a near perfection where many will join as one being in both expression and effect. As if God comes into focus amongst the many by one common goal. Versus when everyone is fragmented and alone in their own just pursuits without a unifying objective at hand. This is when people are the most flawed in their lot in life. By acting as many without a true voice as one total collective being.

God(dess):

The principalities, powers, and glories of Heaven are in a living momentum we call simply as Grace. Or yet we still can call by another name as God's unconditional total Love of all creation. Amen.

--

There is but one one power of God the holy of hollies, and that is to love absolutely. All else in such an absolute love comes the consecrated forms of creation. Manifested abundantly in both life and its renewal in death. The cycles of life consist of a fullness that transcends total comprehension by any one principal to trump any other one. Lest the first cause or reason of being which is God or Love is an embodied truth encoded in the heavens. We come to know of this love through the compassion of our forefathers our ancestors lived for a time and left us this knowing. As I now recall it for you to express as you see fit being in the Image and likeness of our creator God(dess). Amen.

--

For every language that has a word for "Love" has uttered one of the Infinite names of God(dess) in creation. These are among the names of our creator who art in Heaven and within our shared Universe. The absolute creator of all that is seen and unseen in this life and the one to come. Where space is Infinite by the order of magnitude of dimensions and time is eternal in order of scope and distance of a total spherical loop.

Whereby each time you utter by thought, intention, word, and action the meaning of "Love". You have invoked the God of gods into your heart, mind, and surroundings in order to be your witness. No matter if you adhere to a spiritual discipline or not, be it if you have a religious faith or not. For God(dess) is care giver to all his or her own children who conduct themselves in a just manner.

All are welcome to be hugged by the comforting embrace of our maker. Those who state otherwise are selfish or worse delusional in the grips of a power struggle to maintain dominion over others. Absolute Love is a dynamic force not to be discounted as an emotion that is chemical and only biological. It has its roots in parallel in the spiritual realms of reality that transcends the physical. Know this truth and you shall begin to see the unity in all living things, be they of a physical body or not. This is the power that has created our reality, and it will also be the power bestowed on us by a grace that knows no bounds. Be still and feel it within your emotional heart, your logical mind, and your spiritual soul. Amen.

--

An unconditional total "Love" conducted by moderation is the absolute medicine of all our ills in this life as souls. It is also one of the true names of God(dess) our maker. Love is but one of the many names of God(dess), it is a force for good, it is also the very embodiment of God(dess) himself / herself in Spirit. It is a trifold of meanings and of a singular purpose upon creation. To know this is to set yourself free in spirit, and to begin to live a life that is wholesome filled with both benevolence and wonder. Amen.

--

The very nature of God is Infinite and yet inexplicable to describe not just as a mystery unto him or herself. But as an ever mitigating force for change be that change constant or static. In terms of benevolence the Holy Father of all Life is often conveyed by his Divine Love and Holy Light. Yet these spiritual properties also double as forces within the physical realms amongst the living. Absolute Love transcends the biological where those that only consider love as an emotion due to chemical response within the body. Those persons fail to see the relevance of the Divine at work. All they ask for is proof and yet fail to notice that such a Love is the proof. Subtle as it may be if one is not still enough one will miss the handiwork of the Angels like the effects of a quiet breeze. Only those who have an open heart will learn first the truth of how deeply God will love unconditionally our shared creation. Amen.

--

The universal language of life in its myriad of choices is always one of a quiet and gentle unconditional love. A love that is soft spoken, but yet speaks libraries of truth that only a "God of gods" can utter. One that is forever young and yet as ancient as all the creations that are simultaneously ongoing right now across the far reaches of eternity. Our

God is also our Goddess for both genders of mortality are encapsulated into such a beautiful form that allows us to live. God, is not a hoax from the foolish who chase idle hopes. God is an entity that transcends our comprehension and yet is so intimate in our lives we take him for granted.

God(dess), is both the child and elder in all forms of existence upon Infinity. Both silly with a fun loving zest for those who take themselves too seriously. And yet somber beyond a reproach that would be austere anywhere else. My words and my descriptions fail me, but God(dess) does not. We are God(dess) in Image and Likeness not just as offspring in Spirit. But as the very fiber of the essence of the deity himself. We are each a piece of this puzzle we call God the "Great Mystery" that when assembled reveals the most elegant and simple truth of all, we are .....

— —

There is only one love we know as God(dess). All Love in its infinite forms emanates from the very center of God's being. It has always been "One Love with Infinite Expressions". This one love binds all as one blanket of warmth across eternity. In the sweetest eternal embrace for all life through which all the realms of creation may flourish. God(dess) is for all Lovers of any sort as they desire to express their grace within. Amen.

— —

God's, truest form in his Image isn't as a human being. That to humanity is a narcissistic species centric point of view. If it is held at all by those who are shallow through the vanity of the ego.

God(dess), is not in purest form an animal, plant, insect, nor even a mineral or bacteria.

God's, truest form is that of Spirit itself. A Holy Divine Spirit of Infinite Light. That shines within all life forms, no matter their shape, size, mass, or volume.

God(dess), is within us as the "Holy Spirit", and we are alive because of such a divine gift of Life. Amen.

Goodness:

The color of Love is the color of Light, Infinite!

The color of love is often cherished as rosy and pink. Yet, it is more than these two colors of affection known between lovers. All the colors of "Light" akin to a kaleidoscope is truly a radiant rainbow that fosters life in its myriad forms. Just gaze at our Earth and watch as the plethora of life is expressed in radiant colors. A zoological and biological Eden lays before us to cherish and protect for each subsequent generation to cherish yet again.

Light, is often the spiritual pallbearer of Love under the dominion of God's creation. We as the children of this creation that are still learning to cherish and safeguard for the many yet to come. Must do so whenever possible with a delicate hand, taking only as needed and living not in excess to the point of disgust. Opulence is fine, since the Heavens are arrayed in glories beyond comprehension. It is our birth right to live well, but not at the expense of others no matter if they are a mutual species or not.

Yes, be responsible, but not to the point of abusing others in meeting your own ends in this life. Amen.

--

All agents of benevolence act as emissaries for the one we call God the majestic. Acts of grace no matter the scale or scope are not forgotten in regards to the service rendered as a servant or worker of the light. For goodness to be given and received there first must be a sacred intent to be committed in action and thought. Everything else becomes secondary making the good that is brought forth in act and gesture. Having a relationship in terms to knowing what goodness and kindness are in service. Is essential in developing one's being and moral character akin to the evolution of the soul. Amen.

—

Those who say; "All good things must come to an end". Must also realize that all good things will renew themselves in a myriad of fascinating avenues. Yes, good things come and go in our lives. But they come constantly no matter the scale of the goodness from the tiniest form of kindness to the epic miracles that happen every day. If we just become self-aware of the gentle and often sublime presence of benevolence in our midst. We shall know that God's Angels whether as people or in Spirit surround us always. Letting go of how this good should manifest in any fundamental manner allows your focus to be open completely. Being in such a sacred truth provides your life to be uplifted by a child like curiosity. That allows wonder to not only exist, but to thrive!

Be still in such an awareness and follow its synchronicity in your daily life. Gratitude is but one of the many doorways for good to appear. Just be still and it will become a reality in your life always by grace. Amen.

H

Heaven:

Dearly beloved each soul no matter the order of its creation from such an entity of life. Hasn't left its abode and seat next to God the maker.

Meaning each spirit is simultaneously in Heaven and in multiple other dimensions in this one instant. So those experiencing the Earthly mortal guise also have the added benefit of already being saved by grace. There is no need to fret with personal anguish or other persecutions, which are from the vain and troubled at heart. God's judgement is final and unquestioned in his all knowing for all realities. You are home and have never left paradise. Only in your mortal "Mind and Heart" if you will so desire to entertain such chaotic notions according to your own free will. Amen.

Heaven & Hell:

Those who have shared and witnessed a benevolent near death experience are often renewed by the purest rays of God's glory. They've stated that upon gazing into the immense sun like star before them in spirit form they can not and will not look away. The brilliance of such a majestic scene fills one with heart shaking awe. As a soul approaches such an event horizon they are witnessing the entire creation or the totality of God(dess). Once across this threshold of the Holy Spirit one enters the realms of sacred light that are referred to as the heavens.

Yet there is also an obverse sojourn for those that were of no good during there life as mortals. Upon death this process repeats itself but in a backward fashion where darkness replaces light. Awe is converted to horror according to the degree of one's malevolence during a lifetime of wrong choices and wicked disorder. Even in such hellish realms of accursedness there is always an escape for those who truly call out to God in repentance. Since the realm a wicked soul is placed into is one of there own making. And yet such a soul can choose again by the graceful mercy of God that offers instant forgiveness to all souls.

Heaven and Hell are two spheres of the same circle of life. Perpetually a "Ying & Yang" environment that all of ethereal creation is to be known by its inherent properties. Yet both are bound to each other and yet paradoxically both reflect different values of life. Such is the path to harmony for those of us here in physicality that must live by wholesome ideals lest we trip up and end in the wrong portion of the afterlife by default.

Hero:

A hero(ine) is often born out of great adversity that catapults them into the limelight of inner discovery as a rite of passage in life. It is also wrought with anger and pain for the seeming injustice having to be endured for a time. The difference between a vigilante and a hero(ine) is one seeks a blood lust for revenge the other seeks to bring order and balance to the world. The hero's journey is not one to be traveled alone, often times comrades will come along the way for a time and then depart. It is still for the hero(ine) to know this and be able to surrender their true friends in order to triumph. Not in an attempt to lose them without regard, but paradoxically the hero's journey at times is an individuals path as well as a fellowship with others.

Heroes can both serve during peace time and hostile conflicts. They are warriors of an indomitable spirit within seeking to make right wrongs, and not become their worst nightmare in the process. Their journey is both a grand incubator for growth and progress, and an ordeal to be experienced. A Heroes journey is not for the tame of heart and especially of mind. It is for the bold willing to venture where many have forgotten they can tread upon a less used path. Seek first your true purpose and allow the many aspects of character to reveal themselves along your way. If not you will fail, not simply a failure onto yourself but for many untold more needing your purpose in this one life you have right now. Be still and live the righteous cause, not to be a slave of it, but to be a mindful servant of the greater good.

History:

Every generation of people needs to repeat the lessons of their fore fathers. To gauge what is truly theirs to see if they have matured sufficiently as a society. Where history repeats itself as many times with each generation of humanity as needed. Those who proclaim never again the atrocities witnessed are naive at best, fools at worst. Lessons of life are akin to a circle, where each generation of people needs to pass so many revolutions of this said circle of life. To gauge their evolution as entities of God, before all of creation. Than the truth would have set not only a generation free but an entire society for the age to come. Amen.

Holiness:

A person of faith in a benevolent God, using spiritual and religious morally moderated conduct by means of the Holy

Spirit. Shall realize they are flourishing within themselves using the true center of their being. Such expressions are that of: thinking, speaking, writing, serving, and living within the framework of a gracious being.

Those persons that choose embrace such a conviction by absolute love. Will never be forsaken due to their human condition by the Spirit of God within them. The Spirit of God(dess) never abandons his/her own children by the perfect light they journey through in life. Such a Holy Light enfolds us like a second skin akin to an aura of the Holy Spirit.

Go and live for the life of God(dess) within you that is your highest form of worship to him/her. So all may delight in the wonder and glory of the God of absolute love. Where its truest expression in this life of sacred intent is when we live by unconditional love. We choose to dwell in the "Garden of Eden" which we have never left in totality of God's creation. Amen.

Holy Spirit:

The "Holy Spirit" and the "Highest Self" of a particular individual soul are one and the same. Thus they are both considered as intercessory agents of God(dess) for the good of a spirit. They are the bridge to redeeming one's soul from the aspects of a misunderstood world where conflict is preferred to peace and harmony. Only the awakened will benefit from such a distinction that advocate truth above selfish gains. Many will suffer needlessly for not comprehending the paradise to be found within their very souls. Because God is there as the smiling victor of all. By his majesty we live and have abundance be it in a spirit of thanksgiving or the needs of this world which are many. Learn wisdom and allow that to be your guiding hand otherwise your stupidity may become your own undoing. Stand tall not as a wo(man) in a false sense of pride. But as a soul a mirror copy of God(dess) your creator albeit as a sliver in scope and potency. Still all are cherished that remember that God is a loving God. And not one that seeks to instill fear in his own children in spirit. Amen.

--

You are with us, and we are with you. No greater words can be spoken in solace in terms of companionship with the "Holy Spirit". The "Holy Spirit" encompasses all benevolence one may seek in comfort and assurance throughout a daily routine. Be it in this mortal life of ours or in our next life in Heaven. Surrender all your drama and emotional baggage unto the "Holy Spirit". It is a force for good will that can transform your burdens into a wonderful loving grace. Just offer up your permission in order to be touched by the "Holy Spirit" time and again for your own personal good. Set yourself free through the power of the "Spirit of God". Amen.

Home:

Home is where upon your greatest love resides, not in a physical dwelling but in your hearts abode. Some have referred to this as your sacred inner temple. Where it is also your home for your Divine spirit to rest within the bosom of God(dess). Only those who are willing to be open to such a grace of an everlasting love. Will such an opening be made available within their hearts. Letting go of all else but your assortment of greatest loves will you truly set yourself free. Not just with the healing truth but with your dignity of knowing your true potential freedom. The freedom to choose who you shall become with the support of all that is kind and angelic. Where this all begins is within your home where your heart and Love dwells always by Grace. Amen.

Hope:

Where there is love, there is hope. When hope is here so is the fulfillment by joy of what one seeks. By seeking the blessed values of faith in a moderated fashion. One will be led across the highest path to your benevolent intention. For this is the hallmark of the worthy who are open to receive. Amen.

--

What is Hope?

Hope is based on truth, faith, and love for a better event or circumstance to appear. It is based on a truth for the sake of a purity of a true expression in time. It is based on faith so as to have a positive expectation in one's growth. So as to stir within a sacred intention by an outlook that will nourish the soul and not discourage it. It is based on an unconditional Love for the beauty of such an inspired moment that can only come forth by the "Will of God(dess)".

What to hope for is up to the individual in need. However make sure that your hope is on a true foundation based on a faith in God(dess). Not a hope that is based on vanity nor ego, which will only lead your expectations astray. Amen.

Humanity:

One of humanities greatest turmoils is having the strife of slaughtering his own species, or its cousins within the natural kingdom. Be it in the name of survival or justice, by seeking to uphold an order with a viewpoint of extremes. That instills chaos more so as a destabilizing factor, than a common peace. Only when humanity can evolve as a species not as whole but at least a segment of its population. Such a minority will be the ones to considerately herald a purer mandate not to succumb to our physical ape like tendencies of violence. By seeking a higher purpose directed by our divine spirits by re-purposing existing moderate benevolent faiths and philosophies. Finding the Holy common denominator between them all as a construct of an ideal that time has come to fulfill on this chaotic Earth.

The complacency of the majority of humanity will continue by fostering violent ends as a justified means to fulfill agendas. Only the explorers of this new age will not be the lands of the Earth. But instead the lands of the "Mind, Heart, and Soul", which will energize all with humility of their former ways. Justice and Peace go hand in hand, and not Justice and Vindication where barbarism trumps all that is sacred. We are not to fear God, that has been the confusion that has led many to commit crimes of the flesh in his name. We are to be in "Awe" of God's creation all around us, not as its owners but its stewards. Amen.

Humility:

Usually for those of us who are humble we do not always see the fortitude we provide to ourselves or those around us. If we suffer additionally a low self esteem we can undercut our strength and self worth. But, a spiritual inner self love brings us always back to true center. A love that is not of the mind or ego, but of the heart and soul. Offering us a healing balm of pure energy to ease us into our true standing with confidence and conviction. This Love is none other than

God the Holy Spirit in a spiritual form flowing through us. In the most intimate manner of his sensitive compassion to bring us back to wholeness.

Give yourself this Peace, but keep in mind the wisdom of this choice to utilize such a grace in your life often. Doing so will offer you a balance of the "Mind & Heart" that no one person can ever steal or take away from you. Amen.

Humor:

If by all means you can not laugh at your own mistakes sincerely. Than you can not enjoy life as it is all around you. For having a good spirit, includes a spirit of joy and mirth in sharing the happiness of others with others. If one is too serious to care or to depressed to notice than something is amiss. Only a cheerful person can heal him or herself through the comedy that life can all too easily offer. Be open to humor and your peace of mind is assured. Otherwise peace through laughter will not occur, nor healing of ones pain encountered. Be compassionate with yourself and laugh at yourself often and with a good attitude. Doing so will bring humility and wisdom by a grace not usually discovered during common hours. Amen.

I

Inclusion:

Life is a rainbow of inclusive colors of the living. Not the binary thought system of the atypical white and black. When humanity evolves as a species beyond binary thinking into a multiplicity of thoughts. It will have healed itself of poverty and injustice extending its comprehension beyond the "I". Into how it shall affect the "We" be it in humanity or mother nature as a whole. When one suffers, we all suffer be it knowingly or not. When one rejoices, we all celebrate in unison by the nature of our own spiritual identity through God(dess). Amen.

Innocence:

If one is a simpleton or a child of youth one is closest to the bountiful beatitudes of God. Due to the authentic true behavior displayed by joyful glee of a child and of a simple man or woman. In authentic behavior there are no lies, deception, half-truths, guile, or even hypocrisy. One must meet truthful behavior directly and honor it for what it truly is. Otherwise one is not encountering the Holy, but the falsehood of all lies in their lives. That runs contrary to which is the polar opposite to God(dess) the Merciful. Amen.

Innovation:

Simple ideas are God's way of saying innovation is genius and divine.

Inspiration:

Hope, Faith, and Love are a set of Holy precepts that are part of a formula of fulfillment. With Hope comes desire preceding it, where a choice is made to pursue this course with Faith. During Faith there is a silent aspect at work called Intuition or our sixth sense. When it is obeyed again with another conscious choice it will eventually lead to the fulfillment you seek. Where the prize is Love in a heartfelt manner, by remembering that Faith is often by default an indirect spiral path in life. Leading upwards in a Holy conduct through our spirits to "God Almighty" awaiting us with open arms. Amen.

Instincts:

If one insists on following the crowd rather than following their instincts. One will time and again miss out on opportunities and innovative turns for good. Not out of a lack of logic but out of a lack of sheer brilliance according to one's intent.

Intention:

When one truly wants something of value. It is best to blank out your mind. So as to allow your heart to truly speak its desires without confusion. If both the mind and heart speak at the same time. Neither will be heard and an unfulfilled desire continues to haunt oneself. If the mind wishes to speak as to shut out your hearts voice. Than only your superficial nature by logic will speak for you and truly cheat you of your emotional needs. For the heart represents the eternal values of light, love, and life. That illuminate the total truth of the not just the heart, but also that of the mind in tandem. Allowing a sublime solution to appear that will meet your needs and wants as closely as possible. This is considered grace. Amen.

––

Those who hold a sacred intention by unconditional love and have the power to purify themselves. Can achieve any miracle that is sought as long as they take the proper steps to achieve the desired results. That are for the highest grace for all life in terms of following the "Will of God". Those who can realize this wisdom fully can to wonders based on an absolute love for the world and to a greater extent themselves. Amen.

Intuition:

When acting upon a sensation of an intuition or the so called "Gut Feeling". It will often come to a person as a "Hint or a Tip" as a form of guidance. Such notions must be respected and acted upon for the betterment for those involved. Otherwise ignoring your own internal intuitive guidance will be at your own disadvantage. Such "Hints and Tips" will always come to a person in a subtle and gentle manner. Much like a whisper into one's minds eye. There is never any fuss or muss involved in receiving such intuitive guidance. However the results of the breakthroughs gleaned are always profound by their own nature. Amen.

J

Joy:

Pleasure is to the body via our physical senses. Happiness is to the mind where it may appear and linger for awhile. Joy is of the heart where one may express what is truest in one's own nature of well being. Relying solely on pleasure one will warp and wilt away into perversion. Seeking out solely happiness one will become a fickle person. Who if not careful may be saddened more often than being in a state of happiness. Being in a state of "Joy" can be a sacred delight to uphold. Due to the sound principles of expressed moderation of what one enjoys the most in doing. With joy there is duty, dedication, passion, and certainly work. However it is of the most sublime to one's own well being that all burdens just melt away. Amen.

Judgment:

Often in life we judge ourselves first very harshly before allowing anyone else to cast criticisms at us. Much less judging others by our incomplete standards so as to empower our own self-worth. Our standards are incomplete because we are flawed as both an individual and as a species. Our flesh may be imperfect, but our souls triumph over this truth. Because fortunate for all of us God's judgment is always guided by an Absolute Love by default for his creations. Amen.

--

Judgements against others are stones cast at its victims. Victims whom you may not always be privy to their full melodrama. Do we desire to stone a living person as a group to death? I hope not, but we do this time and again by the avenues of the Spirit world. Our thoughts or judgements are like arrows of spirit based harm, shot at others soul through God's eternity. Such consequences we may not fully understand as solely physical entities. With such a centric and divided view point of life by it's own dealings. Lessen your harsh judgements and you lessen the poison you allow into your hearts each day in this mortal world of ours. Amen.

K

Kindness:

Kindness extended is kindness received mutually. It is the beauty of grace shared compassionately that builds upon the Divine in each other. This is the way to fulfilling one's role of loving your neighbor as yourself. A grateful heart can only offer kindness and do so abundantly without reservation. True kindness may be short in a exchange between one or more persons, but it is sublime in nature. Appreciate this fact and kindness will more likely appear constantly around you by grace. Amen.

Kingdom of God:

To see the Kingdom of God(dess) one must look with the eyes of a child. With innocent bewilderment and awe ushered forth with a plain simplicity. So the grandeur of creation to be recognized as surrounding us during this very moment. This awareness is a very powerful reality of the mind and heart enfolded in one instant known as the "Now". Amen.

Kiss:

The sweetest kiss is usually the most intense between lovers. A kiss is truly a lovers paradox. With the first kiss the soul is satisfied, but yet the physical body hungers for more. Akin to seeking an ever deepening bond of a union with our lover.

Thus in our search for the eternal kiss from God(dess). It is as thrilling and sublime as absolute love in our lives. The secret is we never have forsaken our eternal bond with our God(dess). Only in our mortality do we trick ourselves into believing of a separation from our Creator. Our perceived separation through the mind is like a lover asking for yet one more kiss after the last one. However God(dess) as the eternal lover with all of creation is still united with us by the first kiss of life. The first kiss of life is infinite and eternal by its Divine nature of an absolute love. The eternal Lover as God(dess) is united through us all by the first kiss of creation. Amen.

Knowledge:

Where it is said that "Knowledge Is Power". I say that "Wisdom is grace". Whereby combining both knowledge and wisdom into a suitable form we shall invoke great wonders and achievements. That the fruit of such labors will flow so richly and deeply deserved for all concerned in such an undertaking. Do not dismiss good reason, logic, and most of all wisdom. For they are the brothers to knowledge himself. For without one or the other than stupidity is sure to follow. Do not forsake the consequences of your actions only seeking what you most desire. By leaving everyone else to fend for themselves. That is not a responsible steward, that is a pure opportunist without any form of ethics. Guard your intentions and do not allow your core values to be thwarted or warped. For if you do, than you shall surely inherit what perversion you put into it overall. Be mindful of wisdom and his brothers of reason, logic, and knowledge in any endeavor that is worth pursing. All are equally valuable and together they are extremely powerful and a formidable force for change.

––

Technologies can be lost, such is the path of knowledge and discovery. However by the same token wisdom is universal and harder yet still to misplace. Only wisdom can surpass knowledge and its creations of technology to be discovered and lost again. Otherwise costly follies will ensue for those that abandon wisdom in the cause of a pursuit of absolute knowledge. Without judging their actions by foreseeing the consequences of their pursuit through a selfish and vanity stricken ego.

Know Thyself:

As Socrates states so wisely "To know thyself". What this mischievous genius failed to articulate is by exploring ones soul and mind like a cartographer. One will journey beyond humanity and into the Infinite realms of Spirit. Much like our historical explorers of yore seeking new lands and new riches for themselves and their monarchy.

Exploring ones own very self of character will take you to the "Looking Glass" mirror of the Spirit realms (Minds Eye), or what Christ called "The Eye of the Needle". Even before arriving to this looking glass mirror one has to have a strong stomach in resolve. By shining a light of truth where before was only darkness and shadow by ignorance in knowing ones self. Many horrors of self criticism and atrocities that have been committed by your very hands or by the misdeeds of others will need to be acknowledged. But these moments will become less frequent the farther you venture past your ego and into your Divine Soul. By going down the rabbit hole of what is unknown will actually lead you back to yourself within the "Kingdom of God" within your being. Where the darkness of the night will no longer scare you but will uplift you to the wonders that are all about your inner and outer world. Exploring anew with the eyes of a child and the heart of an innocent.

As they say to all explorers to keep the north star in front of you and the winds to your backs. Since the same laws of the natural world will surely apply morally speaking in the meta-physical realms of Spirit.

L

Labor:

Those who choose to take the hard work of another person and claim it as there very own without directing due credit of value to the original person. Has committed two sins (errors). First, they have robbed the true laborer of their handiwork and their joy. Second, the thief has robbed from his or her own self worth. By further causing their soul pain by loss of dignity and compassion to themselves. The one who has been stolen from will need to seek assistance from genuinely trusted persons whom would share their own values.

The thief will be found out not within the usual short term period, but in the long term when their folly will be revealed always. When it is clearly evident they were not the originator of such a well spring of inspiration and intent. By not being able to explain adequately or carry forth the original vision of the work now put forward by the handiwork by all involved. Such is the way by using others as a surrogate in a wrongful manner by not fully realizing the intent of the task to express it with true passion and investment.

Laughter:

The best medicine of the heart and mind is that of a sincere humor that always welcomes laughter in abundance. Laughing at the silly events that transpire in life aids us in gaining an understanding of humility within us. It is a grace best performed in respect of others, but still with a gleeful demeanor that promotes delight. Laughter is best enjoyed amongst friends where rivalry can be enjoyed and often laughed at in earnest. Although any humor at someone's expense may be comedic, but is always by nature in poor taste. Especially if it is cruel in nature and not wanton attention that does nothing to promote goodwill. Be kind, but have fun in your humor by offering it from a place of sincere love and not anger. Amen.

Laws:

Laws are just as dysfunctional as the institutions that write them into being. Laws as a form of social contract are meaningless without an ardent group of people to uphold and enforce them. A law is useless when it is disregarded by the people and especially by the governing bodies that created them. Legal & Illegal reforms are meaningless without a body of supporters to make it so. Laws are a function of the psyche of a society to govern itself, by its own standards of any given culture that dominates it at the time. People are at the heart of mitigating just and unjust laws being ordained or neglected due to complacency, corruption, or a higher truth that is at work. In the end as it is in the beginning, the people are the law and the only authority.

Leadership:

Denying what you do not know as a person to be a fact or a truth. Is the greatest disservice one can do to oneself and within an organization in terms of leadership. Lives and endeavors can easily perish under the weight of such hubris. If one encounters resistance even in the face of a common sense. Than be weary that you are dealing with someone that lacks depth as a person or has his or her own ulterior motivations. Leaders do make mistakes and those that admit such errors shall be the wiser during another similar encounter. Those leaders that are bitter and resentful of others success should be avoided at all costs. For their venom bites the most poisonous amongst all others. Follow those who are worthy with both experience and wisdom. Allow the pretenders to vanish for all they bring is confusion and deception. Know your facts and the truth of the reason of your endeavor. Than you to will succeed where your preparation and execution is well deserved amongst all others.

--

A knowledgeable person alone does not make a leader. A leader is a person whom wills his or her own energies into a format others can adhere to in a decisive action. A solely knowledgeable person does not make a complete and capable leader. An accumulation of facts, figures, and jargon may be impressive in terms of intelligence. But does little in being a successful leader of oneself or amongst others yet still. Leadership is a responsibility not to be taken lightly. However if approached with balance it is as to not become a burden that can not be delegated and shared appropriately.

True leaders are honorable and servants to those that follow them wherever they may lead in a path of dedication.

Learning:

Failure is the merit badge of life because we learn most from our hardships. The lessons garnered from such experiences can last a lifetime. The very act of failing done with the correct perspective. Can be a goldmine of experience paid fully by the toil of our intent. Once we absorb fully the lesson we can transform ourselves like the Phoenix. Whereby the very act of persistence will move us out beyond previous pitfalls onto the road of our success.

Those that have shown us the way are just teachers. In so much we need their good counsel and follow in how to do something correctly. The very best of these teachers will leave an impression that will last the rest of our lives. Where the inspirations they once instilled into us lives on in our character and especially our memories of them. We will certainly have the opportunity to pass onward such past lessons gleaned by our experiences. Where the circle of life by means of learning is completed as we become the teacher to a willing pupil.

Legacy:

The legacy we as mortals leave behind long after our time on this Earth has elapsed. Is that of our kin, be it children, or works for the moments that it mattered, and especially our "Love". Be it a love with a lover, a vocation, a hobby, and especially with our maker God. All of these effects have an importance that will continue to ripple across time and space long after our mortal frames have crumbled back to dust.

Very few of us will be remembered in history of a particular occurrence. Yet still what really is of importance is each other and how we affect our surroundings. This is how a legacy will be remembered if at all. Surrender your need to have to influence those that do not matter in our lives. Only cherish those that an unconditional love is kindled within your bosom.

The rest become the responsibility of our children's, children, to carry the mantle of our success and especially the undoing of our hardships imposed upon them. Amen.

Lessons:

Life has taught us many things, although not all of us as students have chosen to fully pay attention. If we do not choose to pay attention with a heartfelt intent, than the lesson will be repeated as necessary. It's guise may remain the same or differ from each presentation laid before us. Open yourself to a curiosity that will lend to you a yearning to discover for yourselves what is true. By pursuing such a course of action the lessons of life will be easier yet still to digest into your minds and hearts. Otherwise be prepared to be humbled and continue to suffer with confusion until the lesson is understood.

All learning is simply listening with the heart through the mind. That will showcase to you how to pass from one lesson to the next with a steadfast grasp. Reducing heartaches from occurring to the point of causing frustrations that can easily lead to anger and hopelessness. Keep your hearts and eyes open as the truth of life is expressed all around you. Give not into misery, otherwise you will be one step closer to a personal defeat. Look for the "Light of God's" goodness in your midst and there will be the lesson and solution waiting for your grasp to be seized. Amen.

Liberation:

Attachment of any one thing in life that is expressed in excess will grant no liberty. Besides the wanton suffering it bestows on all indifferently for pursuing a path of addiction. The solution is to break this pattern of attachment by using the practice of unconditional detachment in moderation. Doing so ushers forth a fresh breeze of freedom and all things and person to person co-dependencies become less corrosive. By opening oneself to a fuller and wholesome expression of who you really are as a child of God. Not an addict, not ill minded, and not defective. Be still and witness to yourself the liberating power of a inner surrender that empowers and does not weaken. This is one of many truths that can and shall set you free from inner turmoils of attachments to things or people. Amen.

Life:

The journey of life is its own ultimate destination. All souls will always pass this way back unto God as our majesty. No matter the poverty or grandeur in spirit within their might. For life is a path of learning so as to grow fully into our truest birth right. This birth right is not tied to territory of the Earth, it is not gold and jewels, it is not even the prosperity of many children from your own loins. This birth right is of the Holy Spirit itself through us as living souls. Guaranteed by a covenant of promises that are eternal and full of glory for the one that is of a good heart. This glory is of and from God(dess) and not of this world where contradictions abound.

Know this and set yourself free from the reckless actions of a selfish child. Be a King or Queen, but be a true and benevolent ruler over your own desires. Otherwise you will be a slave and a poor one in spirit where only misery will surely follow. For the path to a full and righteous life however you define such a course will lead you back to your loved ones and God(dess). Amen.

--

Keep your mind on solid practical ground in order to maintain a sincere balance. However allow your heart to connect to your soul where the heavens will pour into your spirit. Allowing creative forces to marshal to your aid as a form of awakening your purpose in this one life. Live your dreams, but do so in a harmony with this world that will permit you not only to succeed but to thrive where it is applicable. This is the manner in how to live a life full of grace. According to the eternal promise God(dess) offers creation as a whole. Amen.

--

The act of creating life is a sacred one that mimics the wonders of God our creator. His splendor changes hands and we are imbued with the Holy decree to multiple responsibly. The Holy grace to create beauty in all its forms is both a gift and a duty. The majesty of absolute Love has no end and yet no single beginning. It is Infinite in both essence and substance, because our God is also infinite in both cause and effect. All life is eternal in Spirit due to God being the source or first cause. We as the inheritors of this promise and as the stewards that must follow the course of a righteous form of living. Not merely to help us feel good, but to do good and thus the consequences of good will multiple in wondrous ways.

All of Life be it known and especially unknown to us yet to be discovered by our sciences is in abundance. Like a cosmic "Garden of Eden" the richness is so varied we can easily become overwhelmed if we but lose perspective on the Divine. Stay true to your hearts with the never ending source of unconditional love that God(dess) is pouring out to you constantly. This will ensure a steady supply of both courage and grace to perform wonders all around you. Including to help Life to become prosperous no matter what limitations may be imposed for a brief time. Amen.

——

Our reality and that of the afterlife are one and the same. It is like two sides of the same coin. One side consists of the physical realm of creation. And the other as the ethereal spectral side of life. Neither is greater than the other, they are both different in properties. But yield one unified field of conscious reality expressed as "Life" itself.

——

To have the spirit of youth and the wisdom from age. Is to have used the eternal fountain of life within our very souls. Not for an instant but for a lifetime. Amen.

——

Take life one step at a time and not attempt to jump mountains. Walk gently and you'll walk the most in your lifetime. Compared to all others in this one shared reality we value most. Amen.

––

All of Life is a Circle of events looped unto itself. Eternity in creation is this same loop, but seen from another view point. All in all life is good, due to its multiplicity of constant growth from the grand broad meta-view of the absolute. Still pain and suffering can fully coexist in such a domain of plenty. This inequity must be surrendered for goodness sake. Otherwise a being in life stifles the good that is otherwise there to be received.

Be the Image of the "One" where upon you can rise beyond the noise of chaos. And, into the sublime harmony of the order of a glorious splendor we call "God". Loop your being back into the "Circle of Life" so as to be released from all that is clearly not real in God's dominion. Amen.

––

Those of us that proclaim that life isn't fair. Is very correct, because creation isn't based upon fairness. It is however paradoxically based upon "Love and Fear" in totality. So which aspect of creation do you wish or intend to focus upon?

Living:

The effigies of our lives are living sculptures, for which there is little to compare amongst all. We are living embodiments of other forms condensed into the medium we call humanity. We believe that we have no equals to ourselves and this is where we always err. Life itself dwarfs us into humility, whether we agree with it or not. We are the artists stroke ascending and descending by the curvatures of our lives. We act as critics, but we are truly artists in disguise at least unwittingly from our own intentions. We are Alive!

－－

What is the human condition?

It is none other but a lifetime of pain and pleasure. A living paradox that all life itself encounters no matter the centric view of a particular species. It is truly a universal condition no matter how divorced in emotion a sentient species is from its own psyche. A psyche can be whole or fragmented, whether engineered or natural in selection. It is nonetheless alive and dynamic as a living embodiment of its own ancestors.

It is a universal creation in the eyes of God(dess). Be it fashioned through artificial or biological means what is alive from a neural interface is alive. Our humane definition of living may be narrow but it is not total. That which we can not fathom we discard as either inconclusive or unreliable by means of reproducing such a phenomena. That may suit the purposes of humanity, but be prepared to be humbled when humanity crosses the cosmos.

Loneliness:

For lonely people can have the company of God(dess) the maker of creation. For the grandeur of God can fill in the role of all the much needed relationships. For as much God can shine within you like the torch of life. Attracting to you all the souls that can uplift your mood to a place of harmony. Be calm and know in God's company all things are in order for the lonely of being. That the pain of solitude shall pass to be a fore long memory. To invoke this blessed union with God(dess) all you need is unconditional Love in your heart. In order to grow your relationship with your creator God(dess) forever more. Amen.

Love:

Love is the ultimate absolute magical force known for its benevolence through out creation. Amen.

--

To feel love is to feel united with all of life in harmony. No matter the channel of its expression, ultimately it is the ecstasy that God(dess) must feel infinite times over for an eternity. As one whole manifested being we call "Life" everlasting. Amen.

--

The most eternal form of Love is absolute. It transcends "Time & Space" even beyond the horizon of evil and death. It rides on the waves of the Holy Light of God(dess)'s total brilliance. In both the linear and non-linear thoughts, words, and actions of life that "Ebbs & Flows" into eternity. Amen.

--

Love is bound to no one, it is only bound to itself. The truest form of Love is all sustaining and absolute in its generous nature. Humanity often confuses conditional love and lust as forms of destructive entrapment's. By suspecting that selfish needs through the ego is the culprit. Lust is self explanatory yearning to obtain which it believes it lacks. It is an empty sense of greed from within the deep recesses of the mind and heart. Conditional love is a diluted form of unconditional love. By expressing love with demands plays the petty game of favoritism, where in the end there is no winners.

Unconditional Love plays no favorites, makes no demands, is accepting, embraces all that is good in nature, is inclusive in its purest sense not just in principle, but action and as a force of life. Pure, absolute, total, unconditional, infinite, and eternal love are but a few of the ways to express our relationship with each other and especially with God our maker. Amen.

--

One of the most sincere divine gifts from the most high God(dess) that is given and received in an instant, is the blessed love by grace. Such a Holy Love travels instantaneously because wherever God is, such an abundant eternal Love is there also ready and willing to be received. No mortal can fully conceive the depth and stretch of the good will of our creator. Albeit it is always fun to try to see how far we can reach in our spiritual comprehension. Amen.

--

Wherever your love is, so is your heaven made manifest before your very eyes.

--

Nurture your heart with great loves. For doing so will liberate your life from any limitations placed upon yourself. That shall take away from your Divinity at the expense of your perceived nature as a person and especially as a soul. Allowing yourself to pursue your dearest loves will unleash wonders to begin and to continue to heal your life. Follow your destiny according to the perfect "Will of God" that only you can define in your scared personal relationship with him by a mutual Love. Amen.

––

Divine Love does not discriminate, nor does it dictate the values that humanity should adhere to according to its own free will. Whether these values are of faith or of personal character as to be developed. Love accepts fully the graces that are inherent and the vulnerabilities that every soul has within their own being. Without blame, nor self-righteous indignation to cast out anyone that should not belong. Love that is absolute in nature embraces all of Life as itself unconditionally. Doing so in gentleness and with a firm hand to guide the meek and the afflicted back to wholeness. Amen.

––

To love fully and well, especially unconditionally. Is to usher forth the fragrance of heaven into your life. Heaven can be brought anywhere there is a lover of life. Like the glass blower creating a masterpiece. Love is shaped and formed by the purest of desires of goodwill. Such a lovers grace for ones own divinity can invoke the "Will of Heaven" where glories will be established as needed. That is the power of "Heaven & Earth" in holy matrimony that has moved mountains across the ages of time forever more. Amen.

––

Love when its given truly from within oneself to another. Is by all means a sharing of what is purest in our own hearts. When such a love is unconditional, than it crosses over into the sacred and divine. Our spirits come alive when such an unconditional love from oneself is shared unto many souls. For it is in sharing that we give of our purest essence and life force. As a gift to each other and back to God in an instant by our kind intentions. Much the way God gives to all life with no reservations, we may give to each other in a similar fashion. The circle of Love as God as the inception is completed when we share it with others as we see fit. Amen.

—–

The sublime rests in the most humble of places within our being. It is in such places where the austere is most profound. The sublime rests amongst those who value true love above themselves. In such a covenant there lays the sacred and purest form of sanctity we call absolute Love. Amen.

—–

We are all a grace onto each other if we choose to be so. Otherwise we do not reach our full potential as a child of Spirit. We are all a reincarnation of the one great maker we call God(dess). For that is what manifested life is all about in its simplest form. We are all lovers, for that is why we chose to be reborn as incarnated souls. To love and nurture each other again and again within this great theater we call life the unbounded. We do not only love each other, but just as God(dess) is love itself as a force and power. We are love embodied as well in the Image and Likeness of God(dess). Amen.

Lovers:

When two lovers gaze into each others star gazed eyes. Both Heaven and Earth pass away from their own combined reality. Where entire unspoken symphonies of absolute Love are exchanged to each other. As if a sacred serenade has become beholden in this blessed instant that occurs between them both. This and so much more intensity is the unconditional love God(dess) constantly exchanges throughout all life in creation.

Unfortunately only a minority become Intimate with this form of Divine Love in any given lifetime, although it is always open to all. That is why lovers always tread here in the bosom of God(dess). Or as it is better known as the "Garden of Eden". Amen.

--

When lovers enter into a beautiful relationship for each other sometimes one partner will seek to fix their mate by means of a lifestyle. Often times this is folly unto itself by not accepting the personality or personal character that is the make-up of their romantic partner. Only if their romantic counter-part seeks aid in healing aspects of their life than a fellow lover may help them selflessly. Otherwise turmoil will ensue adding unwanted stress into the relationship. That is masking the possessive controlling personality of the offending lover. Stand back and recognize what is just a minor fuss to an unwarranted intrusion lest you eventually lose the patience and respect from your lover.

Luck:

Being jinxed and blessed in luck are two sides of the same coin. If only the perceived bad luck is looked upon under a new light would one see the lesson to be learned. For a simple shift in mindset can turn bad luck into good luck for your own experiences. Although such a shift in perception is simple in method it is often more perceived as nearly impossible. Not because it is impossible, but due to the sheer resistance portrayed by the one seeking to become more in life. The attitude needs to be altered in order to transcend the negative outlook to one of enjoyment for the sake of self-expression. By having fun in the challenge one will uplift they're viewpoint to a place that the joy naturally rises. Like hot air in a balloon.

We all are what we are by choosing it within our metaphysical soul. That it will only reflect what is on display in our hearts and minds by a neutral fashion. Focus on good luck and your bad luck will evaporate like the darkness upon the light. For good luck is an inherent expression of the soul's Divinity from within. Be it brilliant, sheer, dumb, or good luck all are worthy in spirit. Amen.

—–

Luck is grace manifested by one's very own divinity. It is an atonement to one's personal triumph for that intent amongst the living. Luck is truly the expression of the sublime that binds us all together by blessings and miracles. Amen.

M

Magic:

I believe and know in Magic! This magic is not pagan nor based upon witchcraft. It is based on the sacred

"Divinity" within all of us and the beauty of life itself. This magic I speak of manifests itself in synchronicity, omens, blessings, and most of all "Miracles" both small and large. Another word for this magic is the "Grace" of God(dess) that performs wonders that are dynamic and vibrantly alive. All of life is singing in harmony. It is only when we quiet the turmoil around our minds and hearts by truly listening. Can we begin to hear the orchestra of angels playing for God(dess) in its fullest splendor. Amen.

Manifesting:

There is an old saying we use that, "Seeing is believing". Its second matching phrase is, "Believing is seeing". Allow me to add a third phrase in order to unite them as one statement, "Knowing is seeing in all ways". For our sleeping dream like lives as a world unto itself and our waking state lives as a physical reality is both the same sphere of creation. But under these two states of vibrational living energy where time & space become non-linear in focus as our reality. This is why anything you chose to know deeply becomes manifested as potentiality into our lives. So choose wisely what you select as individuals and entire societies for either way as like a living lucid dream. It comes forth from the ether of a paradoxical creation of the living God. Amen.

--

Those who "Have" will be offered more as to quantify their access to abundance. Those who have a mindset of "Lack" will be given less or nothing at all. Due to an outlook of scarcity akin to a mirror reflecting what is held upon the "Mind's Eye" of such a person. Our Universe is over flowing with abundance able to discern from our hearts and minds what we seek in contrast to our daily lives. So please be mindful as to what you project by your intentions, and do not loose your discipline regarding your desires. Otherwise you shall get more of what you do not want instead of what you truly need. Amen.

Maturity:

Maturity should not be gauged by the age of a person. This assumption can lead to erroneous conclusions of a persons behavior.

A better method is to gauge a person's temperament in a variety of situations and how they respond in those given roles. If by sufficient character or by childish whining or complaints in display of their conduct. This is a simpler yardstick to read a person in terms of their behavior and how they carry themselves around others and life itself.

Medicine:

Melodic music can heal the soul from within its very being of unease. The Ancient Greeks knew all to well that harmonies help recover the mind and heart partially. The medicine to come of Science will incorporate sonic medicine in recovery of various disorders as a form of neural biofeedback. Allowing certain wave lengths to penetrate tissue to undo damage and release toxins in an orderly fashion. Medicine to soothe the beast within is there also to soothe the spirit as well.

Memories:

Our memories whether that of an individual or for the soul of a nation is akin to a catalyst. Such personal or shared memories of a people will illicit the response of the ages long since past. Be they fleeting as a thought or a full remembrance in our mind's and hearts. It is only how we allow them to affect us, can they uplift us, or send us into a deep melancholy of despair. No matter the outcome of such a dependency on recalling our memories as individuals or as a people. What is true, is how we live our lives day to day, be it with dignity or in error. If we err as a person or as a society may we have the courage to know the difference. And, by all that is just and holy the wisdom to rectify it for the betterment of all. Amen.

--

For our loved ones, friends, strangers that have traveled onward before us. Each time we remember and cherish their presence in our lives. We give them life once more in a tender fashion by grace. We make them Immortal in the "Eyes of God" for he has blessed us in our union with our loved ones, friends, and strangers alike. As a singular expression of Life as a whole to be invoked out of joy, strength, wisdom, and most of all Love. Amen.

Mentor:

We often in our lives lament actions not taken and things done that were off-center of our true being. The truth of the matter is these pains we carry all too readily can be surrendered and imparted as wisdom to others. Whether one is in such a role of a mentor or not by becoming the mindful teacher to others with their permission. You can yield noble guidance for those who act on such truths. Where you the teacher are redeemed in regards to your former pain of speculated lost years. Where your pain is transformed into a solid grace that is tangible in your mind's eye and especially your heart of hearts. By aiding another to fulfill their life story in such a way to save them from themselves. For what is saved on Earth is also saved in Heaven instantly where a union or a bond on the soul level becomes transfixed. The mentor and the willing pupil are both reclaimed by a holy kinship that can last a lifetime. Amen.

--

Not all teachers are mentors. Mentors are teachers that excel by going the extra mile with their pupil. That focus not on their weaknesses or their faults. But surmount them by looking beyond to the whole individual with dignity. Where the pupil will eventually rise to the occasion and become a sublime teacher of his or her own to the mentor.

Teaching not the lesson plans, but teaching the mentor who they are as a person. Mentors seek to bring balance within the environment of their knowledge base they are instilling into the student. Mentors teach by example and practice in innovative ways that address the core needs of their students. A good student must be receptive and of a reasonable temperament to be allowed to be guided in many different types of instructions.

Teachers only teach the study material at hand making sure of student comprehension. Mentors truly outshine such basic tenets of learning. Mentors get to remold their pupils by an honorable craft that yields hopefully a better individual for society as a whole.

Metaphysics:

Those of us who hold a strong belief in reincarnation usually tend to believe that it only corresponds to a past linear historical time period. Well it is more than just the past, it is also the present usually known as twin souls.

Besides future incarnations of whatever order of life we become again in eternity.

Another incomplete perception is that a person believes that they are only related in a soul lineage to select individuals. This is not the case, we are related in terms of reincarnation and of oneness with God. For all living moments of the past, present, and future entities be it a speck of dust to other forms of life as souls. What this means is that you can not go ever beyond God nor yourself in the essence and substance of your soul. A soul has no borders in eternity it is both a localized phenomenon and a non-localized being as a living paradox. To awaken to this realization one begins to understand how to access the one holistic archive of life known as the Mind of God(dess). It is accessed via one's ethereal spirit using your intuitive faculties as if it were an open book. In turn one begins to assimilate this knowledge and wisdom with your other mortal five senses.

What can come forth is both awe-inspiring or it can become horrific depending on what the person chooses to access by intention from the Mind of God. It is both an inherent gift and a muscle to be developed like a skill. Such is the paradox into spiritual enlightenment as how many will evolve into ascended masters by grace or descended masters of horror by karma ushered by their personal intentions.

Fear not, all are cared for within the Light as they realize these realities by consistently discovering epiphanies with absolute love all around them. Much like a child in a wonderland of delight and grandeur. God welcomes all to reawaken by the graces of his promise of everlasting life, an abundant journey back home to paradise.

--

We are all mirrors reflecting Life in its totality. Be it in contrast to the sublime as a whole. This mirror has many names, but it is purely just one ideal. Where all things are possible to those who can envision their own reflection with a lucid nature of self. This reflection is benign and non-judging, if one seeks torment than "Hades" is borne. If one seeks "Elysium" than paradise is borne just as well. One can however choose both and experience both "Pleasure & Pain" simultaneously in this wonder we call mortality. But, mortal life is a misnomer due to a lack of foresight into the reality of this mirror we call God(dess), we assume to understand. Much of our mortal assumptions are folly or vain, but the minority of our mortal beliefs of our maker are true.

Seek first your personal creator and all else will be restored to you by unconventional means. Be well and prosperous knowing this eternal truth that shines ever so brightly on us all in this mirror's reflection we call life. Amen.

--

Our Souls are most enlivened when we remember our role as a child of God(dess). Our souls are dynamically active in numerous dimensions of thought, movement, and of being. Our souls are one in unison with each other and the totality of life itself. Be it in time and space or some other relative dimension that binds us all together in Spirit. We are united akin to a grand universal hub that we often refer to as "God". Where all points of life are occurring simultaneously in this very same instant. Even if we under the guise of time by referring to these instances as the past, present, or the future.

Although our awareness is limited by how the "Holy Spirit" of God(dess) functions upon our souls. All is well and in good order as a perfectly synchronized event in a automated fashion. All that must or should be known is that we are vibrant beings of a sacred divine light. That transcends our ordinary functions as mere physical mortal incarnations. We are ageless souls in the Image and Likeness of God(dess).

--

The characteristics of a soul allow it to be in numerous places at once. Such is the inheritance of being in the "Image and Likeness of God". These places can be dimensions of being or of ethereal thought itself. Such numerous locales challenges us to grow in maturity as a spirit. Whereby we travel the spheres of the living, be it in our dream states or during our waking hours.

All of life that is incarnated has a symbiosis with God(dess) in spirit. As extensions of his being whether we accept his "Will" or not. We travel as souls to where we belong akin to a reflection in a mirror. As life is called a school for the soul we sojourn whilst we're alive as people. To multiple places that cause us to grow and mature if we're paying attention in Spirit. This side of creation is a nursery for souls of all phases of maturity. In eternity where their is no mortal age in spirit because we are immortal souls. Again due to being in the "Image and Likeness of God" we can only grow through a process of maturity triggered by life events that provoke depth in us. Thus the "Fruit of Life" is encountered and shared as a gift with other kindred souls in this life.

These places of the soul may consist of fields of pure energy where the formless is given shape by us. The limitations we encounter as humans have no power here. We are limitless without bounds, we are God in infinite variable slivers becoming self-aware. We are the "I Am".

Mindfulness:

Everyday can be a learning experience if we are but open to grow with an open mind from such lessons. If we narrow our focus we are as blind as fools to having limited us of our own options. Not because we are fools, but because we choose poorly in what is in our best interest or that of another person. We need to be truthful to ourselves and be mindful of what we know to be accurate. Otherwise we can make a bad decision worse by not knowing all the facts involved in order to devise an astute formulation. Do not handicap yourselves when confronted with resistance, lest you succumb to defeat before having passed onto the next doorway.

If the world around you is in chaos which is more frequent than not. You do not have to give in and become a lunatic yourself. Stand your ground and observe the cycle of events unfolding all around you. Find your opening and like an albatross fly through the trade winds to your desired objective or destination. Keep a sharp open mind, but even more important keep a loving heart. For having one without the other can lead to an empty existence without a sense of purpose. Amen.

Mind of God:

We are all thoughts in the conscious "Mind of God". All of life created are thoughts of the Divine manifested into various forms of nature itself. All manners of God's thoughts are sublime in both linear and non-linear orders of frequencies. This is the paradox to our shared and combined universe as we currently encounter it within totality. As memories and part of the Imagination of the "Mind of God" we move and having our being in the fullness of eternity. We all have equal opportunity to be benefited or disadvantaged according to how we came to be in this one of many realities.

For those who are called to serve to our highest bidding which is the "Will of God". Have the opportunity to grow fully and have the teachings of truth where ever it may be found. Than as an outpouring of the servants love we bless our surroundings through the vocation of what is good and holy. Not just to be remembered for a generation or two. But to have a positive effect on the needy and the just in nature. To expand what is true and beautiful all around us as a loving mission. For this is not seeking vanity, but seeking the "Kingdom of God(dess)" first that is constantly within our midst.

When we remember this truth we live fully and act upon one of the purest thoughts of God himself. Just as he has enjoyed dwelling upon in thought for an eternity through his absolute love for us. Amen.

--

The Mind of God(dess) is the total and absolute living record of all knowledge and wisdom ever conceived in all creation(s). Such a depository of all life is vital for the growth of all living beings to siphon into their fathomed realities. The "God Mind" has all recorded memories ever experienced by any living being. These memories aren't dormant as in a physical library. These memories are dynamic from the individual authors themselves via a collective of spiritual entities. That has lived them to their fullest scope of the term as in their "Highest Selves". Instead of books the knowledge, experiences, and memories are ushered forth by the souls who lived them in creation. The "God Mind" is accessed within eternity itself as if utilizing a fulcrum within one's very own soul. These resources are always delivered via an illumination of the "Holy Spirit". To those willing and capable of receiving such an awareness as a living vessel in creation and of God(dess). Amen.

Miracles:

Miracles as expressions of God's true being by the graces of his inner "Will" are workings by outreach of his/her blessed host. That can include a variety of actors be it those purely in Spirit or those amongst us in the living. These miracles can come to us in numerous guises from the extraordinary to the sublime in common instances. As the text of "The Course of Miracles" indicates and I quote "There is no order of difficulty in Miracles". What does this mean to us who worship and adore God(dess) in all his/her forms of living?

Miracles are an ongoing process that is unceasing in manifestations the larger ones are recognized by all as if a thunder clap has occurred in their midst. However smaller miracles also known as blessings can be easily overlooked and neglected of the source of such a compassion. How many of you have overlooked a blessing and discredited it as an oddity or a mere coincidence? Than you have overlooked the kindness of a person or an Angel in Spirit that has aided you. We are never truly alone in Spirit and the help that comes to us like a river of Life are such miracles and blessings. Give gratitude to where its due, and know that such movements and gestures from people or Spirit itself are "Orchestrations of the Soul". If the agnostic seeks proof of God than look no further as to the blessings all around you with a keen eye.

For those that believe in separation by the eye of the ego and go without God(dess) in their lives. Will never truly wonder and fall in Love with God(dess) once more in eternity. Amen.

—–

Like God(dess), miracles are a constant spiritual force in our shared universe. Miracles are the eternal response of God's good and Holy Will for all of his creations. A righteous self expression of absolute truth in order to remind the children of God(dess) the glories that are in Heaven. Where the applied metaphysical principles of a miracle is yet another phenomena of the Divine. Which is worth exploring for the seeker of all that is benevolent. The nature of miracles is to unite and bless all in the depths of God's Holy Spirit. Where duality and paradoxes become one law manifested by truth, beauty, and love. That only grace is the eternal marker of a true enlightened heart.

Those who seek life and remember the glory of God first will find their mind's, heart's, and spirit's in a heaven where no ill may touch them in truth. Yes, their physical body will age and turmoils will be experienced all around them. But the steadfast nature of God's love will allow the enlightened to traverse the angst of this world. Onto the roads of the miraculous knowing full well their true place is in a faithful relationship with God(dess) the majestic of all that is true and Holy. Amen.

Moderation:

Moderation is the next best achievement in this life in regards to perfection. For mortals there is no true perfection. There may be a foolish attempt to attain perfection as a mortal incarnate being. But such a spiritual paradox forbids perfection to occur. Such was the intended purpose of living in this physical realm of creation.

Moderation allows for all things excellent to be attainable. Attainable in such a way as to forge open the good or evil as it is intended. Moderation has both good and evil in terms of possibility within such a realm of pluralistic duality. All paths that lead back to God must travel via moderation so as to pass through the eye of the needle. Amen.

Mundane:

For those in paradise as Spirit where the extraordinary is commonplace. Spirit Divine revels with awe in the mundane of our physical lives and the world at large. Such awe is naturally found in children of all sorts as they gaze upon their surroundings. When one of our world realizes such beauty in the mundane. They have discovered the paradise that the Holy Spirit relishes ever so much. As the ones having entered the small and narrow gateway into the Divine. Amen.

Mysticism:

In the Judeo-Christian-Islamic scriptures usually in the books of prophecy there has been stated where Angels stood with many faces. Such of varied beasts, besides of other human like guises in appearance. This has perplexed me how can a spirit have more than one face, much less multiple heads. To offer one plausible explanation is that as like a glass prism of a rainbow. With a multitude of colorful rays of light seen at odd angles. Then these sacred texts accounting of Angels with a myriad of various faces. That were seen through the Holy radiance of their spirits as if a prism was being viewed. Where different and varied essence of these angels was glimpsed in there totality of awe and wonder. This is how the Angels within the prophets vision can be understood in one manner. All Glory be to God the majestic. Amen.

—

All constant forces are the same where "Alpha & Omega" are identical. Much like one entire "Circle of Life" as depicted in the symbolism of the "Ying & Yang" within Eastern philosophies. So our universe and ourselves are Infinite by nature and construct be it down to energetic sub-atomic particles composed of our physical reality. Or up to the very essence of our soulful spiritual identity within God(dess).

Infinity is caused when both "Alpha & Omega" loop seamlessly back unto itself in every growing layered patterns or causeways of ethereal energy. Where one realm begins and the other ends is mere speculation since it is all one. Only science in order to understand must create artificial constructs as if erecting barriers in order to categorize. As time began so shall it end for humanity, but the universe will continue and our souls will continue within God. Be it in this present incarnation or its next reincarnation through another universe be it physical or ethereal. Amen.

Mystics:

God's absolute Love is so bright that it blinds all of creation with his grace. That is what it is like to having remembered the splendor of the Lord God with the totality of his being. Where the "Alpha and Omega" are one and the same as a whole circle of life. Both are identical, but yet both are in opposing polarities going in separate directions. Still following one full course according to the "Will of God" or the fabric of reality itself. The gifts and responsibilities of knowing and acting upon the Divine truth is both a duty and a full joy to be experienced. Not in hindsight, but fully engaged in the present moment. Where the confusion of others with what they declare to be the truth and yet they are just half-truths. Knowing this will lead you on the straight and narrow path along the middle way, between alpha and omega. This is the opening by moderation to know the Divine and the Heavens as a parallel relationship with you. Where the mysterious and wonders of the "Kingdom of God" shine upon you. So you may be in awe and thanksgiving of the life you so richly deserve through God(dess). Amen.

N

Nations:

Both cultural and political willpower upon a society to better itself can occur only if the leaders and visionaries appear. Otherwise inertia will take hold forcing an entire society to lay adrift. Being predominantly at the mercy of the crashing waves of inaction. Causing ripples upon ripples of consequences that leave a society further weakened losing its ethics and convictions as a nation. No nation can succumb to such a fate without the implicit consent of her own people.

As the saying goes if good men do nothing than evil will flourish. Than if good leaders of the land do nothing than a nation will perish. In its place will rise its evil twin if safeguards aren't cherished for the masses at large. Any bordering States will be sucked down to a crashing society like being pulled under by the churning of a whirlpool. Profiteers both foreign and domestic will be the vultures to pick apart any remaining meat on the skeletal remains of a society that has fallen.

All of this can be avoided if the leaders and visionaries of the land. Support the people truly without regret nor poor excuses. Any false leaders will be shoved aside allowing the brave ones to take the lead. Societies must remain vigilant to the will of the people or all shall die a slow death. Only to be remembered in the history books as a cautionary tale.

Negativity:

For those who are devout cynics, pessimists, and naysayers where the glass is unconditionally half empty. The lens they choose to view the world through is seen constantly filled with struggle that borders on insecurities and with doubtful recriminations. Their cornerstone mantra is "It Can't Be Done", and so it becomes law to them with antagonism. They have given up on the dream of a good life, if not a greater life. They choose failure over success, because it it safer for them not to take another risk. They may have been abused by another or may have hurt themselves traumatically to the point of shrinking from the world.

No matter until they choose to change their ways for their own personal good. It is best to always avoid these sort of souls who have held up and destroyed the dreams of others. They have throughout time shunned the beacons of hope, and inspiration to them is as foreign as a sincere love. They have wrecked the noble dreams of many great souls. Steer clear of them until that time one by one they realize the pain they have caused another. Live your life independently from them, even if it means that emotionally you aren't as willing to share your dreams out in the open. Because they will trample your dreams like a stampede of horses with no regard to the sensitivity of the subject matter. Be it to maintain dominion over you or to maintain their agenda for your personal life to come. Empower yourself and set yourself free from their ruthless grip of control over you. You deserve it, because humanity needs your talent and brightness to continue to shine in our shared world. Amen.

Now:

As it is said to enjoy your journey in life. But in a modern world where time comes at a premium for most. It is best also not to arrive as if a martyr to your destinations in life. By being exhausted in both health and sanity at each turn that life may offer us. Keep your awareness centered in the all pervasive moment of "Now". That is the best rule to enjoy the time along our journey in this life and the next one to come with God(dess). Amen.

Objectivity:

The subjective thought is inherent to the human spirit. For without subjectivity humanity would be divorced from his or her own soul. Albeit objectivity is a must in maintaining order otherwise chaos ensues with a purely subjective mindset. Although a harmony needs to be struck between the subjective and objective capacities of the mind. In that the "Kingdom of God" matures in its own grace by the deeds of a balanced outlook of the faithful and the secular. Amen.

Obstacle:

When an obstacle has been encountered in your life. Know that in each difficulty therein its core is a solution to be found and worked out. However many people give up by inaction only to be swallowed whole with despair. Others yet still choose to self medicate through destructive addictions to numb their own pain. Where by they dig an even deeper hole of despair unwittingly. The best path of resolution is the constructive path that allows for inner personal work to be accomplished. No matter how slow the pace or if there are "Fits and Starts" to a solution. Patience, hope, and unconditional love are the keys to unraveling any difficulty under the sun. Be it big in scope or trivial in consequence. All can become better with thoughtful persistence that allows one to overcome and not despair. Amen.

Oneness:

I am (We are) a mirror to all life since we all express universal qualities no matter the species or expressed order of life itself. We are all truly one in essence and substance with our Creator God the Supreme Unifier of our universe.

––

Some say that "He or She" is my soul mate or my twin soul. Well the truth is rather stranger than fiction by such a meta-physical distinction. We are all "One", united by Spirit there is no separation in the Eyes of God. Only in our mortal human musings heralded by our fragile egos do we state that such and such is our soul mate or twin soul.

All universal properties of the Spirit be it of character or disposition are embedded into our soulful DNA. It is such a spiritual DNA that binds us as one meta being in a macro sense that we call God(dess). We are no more foreign by spirit to one another than we are strangers through the lens and filters of our human egos. We are "One", if we wish to complicate this truth with fanciful terms of soul mates or twin souls. We do so at our own disadvantage and ignorance and thus lose something in the translation of this half truth.

––

When it is spoken that we are one in spirit with all life as souls in a macrocosm. Another insight to help see this vantage point of understanding is to know that all past, present, and future life is a reincarnation of yourself. And, that you are a reincarnation of all that was, is, and will be again as the entire scope and breadth of the Spirit of God that is in your being. Be still and welcome this understanding, and make your peace with it. Offering thanksgiving that your awakening continues toward all that is pure and of sacred importance. Amen.

--

We are all beacons of God's love. Only we who choose to express such a holiness grow into a radiant flame of life as blessed beacons (souls) of God's good graces. Those who choose to pick up the mantle of God do so with a distinction of an inborn divinity that does not divide, but unites us as one. The good news of the Holy Spirit is not meant to be carried as a burden or cause denials where their should be praise to God. It is to be carried like a gentle fragile package that when delivered as a true gift. Blesses both the giver and receiver instantly without discrimination of whom is worthy or who is not. It is total, akin to being enveloped in the radiant love of God's good nature. So be way showers, become beacons to light the way for your siblings in spirit both man, woman, and all manner of creature that has an inborn capacity to love. We are one under God and we shall not be separated from his absolute mercy. Amen.

--

When we seek the "Kingdom of God" within our very own spirit. We are reaching into the being of God(dess) that is in all life. Such an act is both sacred and holy as a loving response in worship. Since it binds us to the meta consciousness we call the "Mind of God". Where all living beings be it in flesh or in spirit are one. In a shared response of life in whatever reality we may find ourselves within. We are not separate entities as opposed to each other. We are bound up together because God is the force that binds us together as one. Such is the out pouring of God's Absolute Love allowing the very essence and substance of life to be united in both spirit and in a mutual love. Amen.

--

We as souls of the one master creator are all beings of unseen light waves. A sheer spectrum of living light that encompasses the whole of creation. Our Spirits are like a reflecting prism of living light as ethereal energy. As such we are mirrors of the creator by which we can co-create like in his or her own image and likeness. Keep mindful of what you reflect with your very own personal soul, since by extension it affects the whole universe. As a cycle of what is reflected outward eventually orbits around the globe back onto us as karma. Make sure what your core ideal is worth the energy you've invested into it for all our combined sakes. Amen.

Oversoul:

Our souls acting out as an incarnation of our "Highest Self" or known as the "Over Soul". Will inhabit various dimensional planes of existence be it from the numerous ethereal realms down to the physical common reality we describe as life. Consider "Space & Time" as if a geometric circle representing our evolution in the span of a lifetime. Our "Highest Self" as a witness absorbs all of our stages of a mortal life. Be it our mothers womb, our physical birth, our total life, and our return to Spirit in passing from mortality. To us, such a life can be blessed by many decades of a linear time line in one or more regional landscapes. To the "Over Soul" all of this occurs in a realm without time nor space as a dimension. So all this occurs instantly like a compressed reality akin to a fast forward playback recording. Similar as to how those with an experience of their life flashing before their eyes near a life ending hazardous encounter.

Now consider a multitude of our twin souls, who are a mirror Images of ourselves having incarnations in other time lines within the space time continuum. Be it as humanity in our ever present world or other lifetimes that are to be perceived as bizarre from our vantage point. Why this occurs is that God is hedging his bets in order to experience all realities be it our own or parallel ones. In order to be a fully living dynamic deity worshiped in either monotheism or an assembly of deities. So as to experience the totality of creation through his or her own creations. Not as a Divine puppet master, but as a loving parental figure that transcends fickle curiosity into the sublime affections of all life. Be such a life in flesh or in spirit as an entity living at large within creation. Amen.

P

Pain:

Pain is both a catalyst for growth by healing and a force for suffering. It is up to the participate to choose whether to heal by opportunity and to grow by transforming for the highest good of all. Or to succumb to suffering and surrender all faculties to being wrecked in life. Pain is a instrument and an effect to overcome or to be acted upon. Choice is always at hand to the naive mind or the mature mind of an entity at the crossroads of pain. Amen.

--

Passion:

Every one's path is an individual creation unto themselves. However what they seek is as universal as our beloved creator God(dess) has offered to all life. A blessed paradox to be experienced and to be pursued for those who seek a fuller life as a soul. No one should dictate to you what is in your heart as a vocation. They may be angelic in helping you discover your talents and passions. However this is different than becoming a tyrant in divorcing you from your highest good. Be mindful and curious as to what heaven is beckoning you to discover about your own self. When you do commit yourself to your own souls calling. Both Heaven and Earth shall celebrate for another prodigal child has returned to paradise. Amen.

Peaceful:

To be peaceful is not always to be right. To be peaceful is always by a mutual consent with yourself and your maker God. Where acceptance calms the waters of your mind's sense of separation from the world. To be peaceful is to honor your neighbors actions as your own in so far that we all are one in Spirit. To be peaceful is to enlighten your view of the world not just through yourself, but through all life on our shared reality, no matter the origin of the species. To be peaceful finally is to accept yourself as a whole being and not a fragmented one. Amen.

--

Those that seek righteousness through the ego will only find hardship. However those who seek unconditional love in a moderated fashion will find abundance in a myriad of outlets upon them. Being right is not always the best use of truth. When having to be right and thus making others wrong. Is a trick of the human ego in finding superiority, no matter if it is an illusion by disguise. Compassion is the root of all healing of any truthful or perceived wrongs. Since compassion is of love and love an extension of truth itself.

Being loving instead of being right all the time. Lends itself to peace and an abundant peace without the need of logic nor reason. This is the core path of being a peace maker and by extension the essence of a benevolent diplomat. Whereby acting as an ambassador of the supreme truth of God(dess) within all of us who are created in God's own Image and Likeness. Amen.

--

Only those that make peace shall have peace of mind. For in the creating of peace there is a solace of the heart and mind that surrenders logic for calm. A calm that only those who know how to be still within their mind can be open to many wondrous things. Peace for its own sake is empty. Peace when it is shared is truly lasting and harmonious. Surrender your havoc and know the healing fortitude that a gentle peace can only offer through unconditional love. As both an act of gratitude and a surrender to a higher power at work in your life and circumstances. Amen.

Perfection:

The human ego always seeks to be right and be in its important state of mind. In its own folly and rigidness any sort of behavior becomes warped beyond comprehension. A truer spirit of dignity may never be found by the limited beliefs that the ego promotes itself above all else. If perfection is to be truly sought by the mind of a person driven by the ego. He or She must truly surrender the power of a mental self gratification of the ego. To pursue the sublime "Will of God" that by the nature of God is far more omnipresent than you could ever achieve as a mere mortal. Assume the graces of the "Holy Spirit" and soon you will realize that seeking perfection in a mortal guise is folly and an error. It does not exist in physical form, only excellence by means of moderation can the next best thing to be achieved. Only through our souls as God(dess) as our benefactor can we be in a state of perfection due to being in the "Image and Likeness" of our creator.

Be still and realize such a truth through humility by means of prayer, meditation, or contemplation. All else of the ego is limited and flawed as is its nature by default. Only by assuming your role as a Diving being can you surmount your difficulties through God who is in Heaven and within your hearts by an unconditional Love. Amen.

--

Our souls are complete and perfect in the Image and Likeness of God(dess). Paradoxically our mortal guises are flawed by imperfections be they genetic in nature or based on our own moral failings. Where we should only strive for excellence in all of our on goings as our highest intent as people. This is the contrast and difference between what is Divine and what is clearly mortal in shape and form. Amen.

Persistence:

A steadfast persistence always goes hand in hand with the fulfillment of our desired intentions. However this persistence I speak of also needs moderation so as to flourish into our eventual goal or objective that we seek. Otherwise one can lose focus and balance by overextending ourselves in a forced manner. That warps us from our true desired wants and our dreams. An inner poise is crucial especially when we begin to doubt our resolve. This doubt is no friend, but only fear based ills that are preexisting that you harbor. Do not feed them with attention, if you do you shall continue to spoil your promise to yourself and if not onto others you care about.

Maintain a self-discipline that is honest knowing your boundaries. When one loses focus it begins by over doing one thing or another to the point of a sheer madness of micro-management. Allowing yourself to breathe and "Let Go" of the tiny details. Only concern yourself of the "Big Details" and let the rest work itself out in its natural order. Like a loaf of bread in the oven the yeast within your plan will take hold and grow. Do not fuss like a over zealous maternal figure. Be still and watch how like an astute parent you watch your dream or goal blossom into maturity. This is but one path to self-fulfillment under the sun.

Personal Development:

The greatest rule to personal development is to rule over oneself entirely. By not willingly seeking to thwart or confuse others to follow you just for your own selfish pleasure. Be they loved ones, family, friends, co-workers, and strangers alike. Yes, it is true all organizations be they civilian and especially military. Have a structure and utilize a hierarchy as a chain of authority. But, I am speaking more about personal development as a mature and responsible adult. In ruling over yourself means to know your own being fully. Not just on the surface by your own superficial likes and dislikes. Just truly knowing yourself as a person and especially a soul. How you behave and how you respond to the challenges and joys of living. How do you succumb to fear and how do you rejoice with the most sublime love. By knowing your own virtues and understanding your faults be they vices or neurosis. You shall "Know Thyself" as the ancient Greek philosopher "Socrates" famously stated.

In knowing yourself, you shall more readily rule over yourself with confidence. By understanding your limits and boundaries as a person. Where you can push yourself as a challenge and where to respect your limits and leave it alone. True men and women of righteousness know themselves needing not to manipulate others to their selfish whims. They lead by example not to coerce others to do their bidding, but to show others a better way. Those who grow as people also grow their inner soul as a testament and glory to God. Where the peace of the world may be in doubt. But the peace of a person who knows themselves truly is to be strengthened always by grace. Amen.

Pestilence:

Humanity can never truly eradicate death, poverty, hate, discrimination, racism, terrorism, nor diseases of all kinds. However humanity can influence the outcome of such a pestilence in the orders of scale. By focusing as a collective meta-being on healing such pain from the Earth. Otherwise we may speak mightily in terms of freedom & liberty for all. But we will have become hollow losing sight of what is most precious, which is each other as living souls of God(dess). Amen.

Philosophy:

With all the sciences of our species here on this Earth. We always seek out the perceived truth of ourselves and our ever stretching environments. Such passages in understanding of a scientific mind is both judicious and a methodological complication to the uninitiated mind. Even for those with a grasp to one or more scientific discipline of study. Having literally what seems as a sub-domain all their own in culture and professional language. Having said this and what is done in the name of science in regards to the most climatic response to each other. We often fail to realize the philosophical or metaphysical quandary we have been placed within. Seeing the grandeur of this creation without a faith lacks a depth of what does it all mean?

Those with a spiritual faith are comforted and assured in confidence that the grandeur found in science has a meaning. The purpose can be made apparent if the schism between science and faith is forgiven. Allow the "Bad Blood" to wash away, not in a total embrace. But, in respect of how the other seeks to justify their reality in a perceived truth. One truth quantified by repetitive observation through the means of science. The other in truth by hope, faith, and love in what will be. This is a paradox, but it doesn't have to be an impasse somewhere in the middle of the two.

--

The physics of any given reality, be it the reality all around us or the reality of our souls substance can be viewed as contrary poles of existence. However it is and has always been one reality, albeit layered into several dimensions of creation.

We as humanity can be in denial to the prowess of our souls environment, and still adhere to the macro dynamics of the physics of our world and the stars beyond. This is still a short sighted approach where science creates an artificial conflict with spirit. There is no separation, it is all one family of understanding. Only in our ego's and immature sense of justice can we say otherwise, and declare it as the ultimate truth to our own disservice.

Playing:

To play is to live in its most simple and yet profound manner. In shaping who we might become once more. Being able to play allows us to act out our unresolved tendencies from the place of the abstract. Playing affords us the luxury to act in a near safe environment and to grow by its outcome for the better or worse. We can learn and be enlightened whilst we're in the center of playing. It is where fascination and wonder meet experience head on in parallel percussion. To play is the act of consecrating the common and the profound in one instance. And, yet keep going without looking back nor having a care of the world at all. It is the abode of the sublime and the stage of the dramatic in all of us. Amen.

Polarization:

When a society is divided from itself by divisive ideologies, Lo and behold its own undoing is at hand. Inviting an atmosphere of polarizing behavior that becomes uncivilized and hateful. Where only the fundamentalist view is the true view by those who have become distorted in rhetoric. Such ideologies can be from the secular to the religious in nature and action. Causing only those with exclusive license to spew their bigotry without pause or concern for the public good. All others whom are not of this elitist thinking be they foreign or domestic in citizenry are to be mistrusted and alienated.

Such a path of beliefs will only spiral downwards away from peace and democracy. Leading to civil eruptions be they protests or riots that are violent and antagonistic. Instead of seeking the "Middle Way" of compromise and a compact of a declared public trust in good faith. We will experience ruin in all its chaotic forms until we seek not to bleed and to hate no more. Nurture instead a spirit of cooperation and compromise to be truly peace makers and not victims of discord.

Politicians:

Be wary of political leaders that use fear tactics to herd their citizens to a consensus. For no good is occurring by seeking to ambush the naive of heart turning their ideals against them. Rather than heed those leaders within the leadership of an organization. That propose notions of inspiration that bind many into a common cause for a greater good. This is the difference between a cheating hypocrite and a Shepard of true ideals and values. Amen.

Politics:

The nature of the political beast within us isn't so much of not agreeing with others. It is in maintaining a degree of respect that is hopefully mature of all participates involved. For if the body politic is at a loss. Are they not representative of us as a whole at least in a republic democracy. If we elect poor leaders to office that have no other vision but just to be re-elected to political office. Than we have failed ourselves more over than electing idiots into governmental office. May our angry not overtake us as citizens by the clumsy and all too often ineffectiveness of politicians. Some outrage is a good thing, but outright hostility is contagious and poisonous to a society at large. If we seek to improve our lives than God help us if we over rely on our politicians. To do all the heavy lifting without the help and input of the citizenry to hold them accountable.

Prayer:

Prayer has a power that it functions and dynamics can transcend time & space together as a form of grace. This potency of grace we call prayer can even transcend spatial historical events. For those of us who reflect on the past, be it on a personal or impersonal scale. That such a form of prayer we call as a "Blessing" can be delivered to the all points within time, be it the: past, present, and the future. Even beyond our frail understanding of such dimensions of existence can we influence. Albeit slightly the impressions, conditions, circumstances or our lives or those of others. Just allow the Holy Spirit to move through you as a Divine principal. And await a confirmation by synchronicity to know that the blessing was received fully by God's grace and Love. Amen.

— —

When we pray to God(dess) for a desired outcome in our lives or the lives of others. We often expect an outcome to be done via a specific manifestation. This is an error on our part, for once we dictate the terms of the yearned occurrence. We have spoiled the request for the Holy Spirit to carry out by its mysterious ways. When we pray to God we must make sure that request is benevolent and in alignment with the "Will of God". After that step is set in motion by intent, we must pray as if what we have asked for in prayer has been set in motion to becoming a reality. Than we surrender the prayer as releasing a dove into the air and thus we avoid suffocating the prayer request by our worrisome ego.

Allow the prayer to flow to its intended destination. All prayer that is earnest using the catalyst energy of unconditional love through our mind's eye. Will launch the request like a projectile directed to the Holy Spirit. Oftentimes daily affirmations that a prayer has been fulfilled with thanksgiving is in order. This will replace the mind of the ego from worrying and allow positive reinforcement of our affirmed expectations to be fulfilled. But, remember do not dictate the terms of the prayer request to God. Just allow it to free flow by the grandeur of his mystery to enfold your prayer by absolute love. Amen.

Prosperity:

Often those who seek wealth are told to enrich their attitudes using a belief system of prosperity consciousness. But what does this mean to one who truly is foreign to its concept and dynamics? Basically it is molding the infinite spiritual energy within their being to work in parallel with the laws of metaphysics expressed in moderate conduct. In turn they will prime the pump of their soul's worth by allowing the gentle flow of: love, compassion, dignity, trust, and faith to pour all around them. This prosperity is not just of the material riches but of the Kingdom of God(dess) that is on the scale of eternity. Spiritual soulful prosperity must always come first by default. Otherwise vanity will short circuit the path to any form of material success that is of lasting value for the good of all. Amen.

--

When so many of us think of prosperity, we picture finite material goods of this Earth. True prosperity is unconditional, which stretches itself into areas of soul consciousness. Such as the well being for one's health, one's relation with others, and one being able to give unto others. By doing so without tying poor conditions to the act. These are always the first fruits of true prosperity when one see's the blessed constantly around them. All else in material needs and gifts is the gravy on top of the meal, and not the meat of the main course dinner.

—–

For what one person seeks they must exchange the same quality to another so as to gain it within themselves. This is the path of creation allowing prosperity to be gained as it is shared with one or the many. This is the "Circle of Life" most apparent by virtue and in deed. Be mindful of such a duty to oneself in order to allow greater things yet still to take hold within your being. This is the way to ensure the riches of Heaven and Earth grow without measure. Do not lust for such gains or they will become fleeting. Be sincere with altruistic thanksgiving and they are yours always. As in spiritual truth they already are according to the "Will of God". Amen.

—–

Whatever you seek to attain you already possess within your very own personal soul! For your soul is a fragment of the whole Spirit of God(dess) the creator of the universe. Just focus with gratitude on what you seek to attain. Then with gratitude in your own heart begin to take simple practical steps towards your goal. Over many moments of patience you will attain or arrive at your desired destination. Just do not give up! Give yourself relief with unconditional love when you begin to fret with grief. Surrender all that garbage of stressed emotions to God(dess) fully. Allowing it to be recycled into a grace your able to receive by your own self-imposed limitations.

Act upon each sensible opportunity as if it were a doorway into the next room in God's mansion. Sooner than not your realization into fulfillment will be arriving with your appropriate acceptance. Give thanks in advance with Love not worry in your hearts. For in spiritual truth you are already a god in spirit. Not as "Thee God the Creator", but a god(dess) or child of the creator. The "Spirit of God" can achieve anything through the one that has a sensible faith and trust in the Divine. Amen.

Providence:

Providence and Grace are both twins and as sisters their efforts are to unite creation with itself. For creation filled with so much mortality can cause rifts to appear that need to be healed time and again. Since every generation of Life marvels at the splendor of the stars in heaven. They forget that they are these same stars but they're heaven is in Spirit. Not of the world they may in habitat just for a moment from the blink of the eye of eternity. The work of providence and grace is not easy, but it is well meaning and so filled with an absolute love. An absolute love just like from their father whom we call God.

Providence and Grace may be lesser goddesses or arch angels yet again to others. But they safeguard us from ourselves and in so doing maintain a union between the sisters that is so precious to any observer. That just so happens upon them for another moment in eternity. Amen.

--

Providence travels forth like a rainbows arch into the being of those who permit it to move them beyond their own horizons. The nature of providence is to shift ideals of meaning that are true and blessed by manifesting them into our reality. Where upon the results alleviate hardships that would've occurred otherwise by stubborn and misapplied determination. Be still and know that "Providence" is the sister of Grace's handiwork in all things true and beautiful. Amen.

Purpose:

The journey of life is to realize who we are, by what we do and can become for it.

––

Sex without an orgasm is an empty act of self-gratification. In so much that life needs love to survive. Conviction without merit is meaningless, there is no in-between. We must either soar with a zeal or we fade into the neutral gray background of the status quo. We each define our lives differently, but we all experience it universally. We need to bind ourselves together so that we can unleash the living dynamic soul within us. Otherwise we fade without merit or a lovely muse to guide us onward to a fuller life.

––

For those who seek a lifestyle of meaning served by purpose than listen well. To live rightly is a grace from God(dess) of the Most High. Albeit it is not meant to be an easy feat either in its pursuit. To live a life of well being one must find a balance that is appropriate to one's own purpose in life. Once found and understood correctly, then one can live by such a hallmark of fortitude. Otherwise one will wander far and wide in a haze of confusion not valuing themselves truly. Find your balance and it will lead you back to yourself and God(dess) awaiting you with open arms. Amen.

Psychic:

It has been stated that God provides an inheritance for those who seek out the Kingdom of God on this Earth. Such a blessed kingdom resides within our spirits as like a dimensional doorway to the soul. Our Divine inheritance takes many sacred forms of life. One such set of manifestations is our spiritual psychic abilities that is a baseline in all life. Only the distinction of magnitude of such a sub-set of psychic abilities is a known factor of our latent Holy gifts within us.

This will only depend on us if we truly acknowledge these God given powers and begin to utilize them as natural inborn talents. Where over a course of a lifetime we grow spiritually not because of these powers. But because we have worshiped God(dess) rightly so in all forms of benevolence accessible to us in this life. Amen.

—

Psychic abilities are the soul's tendency to flex its ethereal muscles per say. Such psychic attributes are for the awakened soul to utilize for the common good of all. Albeit it can be exploited to disastrous effects to the point of no return venturing into the mindset of insanity. Moderation is key with harmonious balance in utilizing such primal influences during personal psychic development. Psychic protection is but a prayer away in visualizing the Divine white Light of

God(dess) shining upon you like a beacon of grace. Whereby invoking the Angels to come to your aid no matter the need in question. The angels are but a breath and an intention away from responding to you with an unconditional love. Amen.

R

Rainbow:

Our souls shine brightly like a rainbow of life. Where we are accompanied by many spiritual elements throughout our sojourn on this Earth of ours. In Spirit we are never alone, we constantly have the blessed company of our loves ones. Be they known to us in this lifetime or if they have been with us in numerous lifetimes. Each spirit acting as a "Ray of Light" shines its own brilliance of a holy light within the "Rainbow" of our life. We are united in a common purpose, wherever we go be it safe or not on this Earth or beyond. Our heavenly companions surround our spirit as if a constant bubble of absolute love that only the "Holy Spirit" is capable of producing. Those that accept such a rainbow of heavenly unity shall walk in peace and with the grace of God(dess) always without fail. Amen.

Reality:

Our reality is but an echo of our mind.

Recovery:

When we blame ourselves we cut our divinity from its own source. Beginning to short circuit our belonging to a right sane mindset. We surrender our own humanity by burdening our being with faulty sick thinking. This is where surrender of such a blamed mind needs to be conducted. As a form of willful healing of a split mind & heart. Using forgiveness when one is truly at fault, and not just assumed to be in error. This is the path of self recovery and realignment of who we truly are by a sacred purpose for our own highest good combined. Amen.

Redemption:

Evil in all of its incarnations be it brutality in the physical forms. Or other forms of abuse be they emotional or mental anguish conducted purposely. May not always be best in a spiritual sense to fight "Fire with Fire". For redemption and fostering in a sense of harmony once upon all souls. A greater peace or unconditional Love must be offered first through various acts of forgiveness be they personal or societal corrections. Spiritually speaking we do not fight our way to paradise. We do heal our way to heaven with the purist holiest of hollies by a Divine Light of our creator God(dess). This is the catalytic force described by "Jesus Christ" when we do good unto our enemies in order to improve ourselves. Setting a path to reconciliation where the truth guarded by the righteous sets in motion miracles upon families and a society at large. Amen.

Reincarnation:

Our souls have never left our place near or within God(dess). We that come to be reborn in the physical world are here to love and be loved. To evolve by Grace unlimited if we so choose to by our own consent. Otherwise we are free to wander creation for our good or ill. Our only standard is to live fully and wisely by unconditional love. Such a goal leads us back to our source God(dess) in Heaven. Where permitted we grow deeply in this life by living well with each other. Amen.

Relationships:

Being in a romantic relationship with the wrong person is like a troublesome medication. It will offer heaps of horrific side effects not expected in common hours. Needing a physician of the heart to help one have the courage and resolve to move on with their own life. Away from the offending partner causing an illness of the mind, heart, body, and spirit. Once invested into the wrong person it is harder still to leave such a relationship without pain. If abuse is prominent harder still is the extraction from such a toxic relationship. Needing the aid of one's own support network of contacts for strength and courage. In order to live a fuller and better life as you truly deserve as a child of God(dess). Amen.

Religion:

All sacred benevolent paths are valid movements towards God. When one has the outlook of an all inclusive universal reality. This is however the very open minded flexible attitude that isn't shared by everyone. Where some can be angered to even mention such an option of possibility. Those are clearly the ones who have an outlook of an exclusive path to God. The paradox is that both stances are correct, since it's usually different stages of evolution in worship towards

God. Neither is more righteous than the other, both will lead to God in the end and to a new beginning. Amen.

--

For those who discriminate against other benevolent faiths or philosophies would also invalidate their own. But for all of a moment until a distinction is drawn upon. Which is how can God's Holy infinite Love, Life, and Light be restricted to only one religious or philosophical doctrine. Throughout this present day period across the span of our macro scaled physical Universe can their only be one chosen people? Doing so interjects an evolutionary primitive throwback mentality that limits the grace of an unconditional God head. Since our maker God(dess) is never a conditional deity set upon narrow minded principles that excludes the totality of his own myriad creations. His or Her own absolute reign envelopes all life be they small or near god like in presence. If any faith or philosophy excludes another than it is done so at their own jeopardy in denying another incarnation that is representative of God(dess).

--

All the places of worship are sacred Holy places to God(dess) and his / her Divine host. God(dess) does not distinguish between religions or grants one more favor than the next one. All are the same to him and her since they advocate the Holiest Spirit above all else. No matter if God(dess) is seen as one deity or a pantheon of deities. The one we call God(dess) is and can be viewed in numerous aspects all united as one majestic Divine diety. Where the virtues of benevolence are held highest is where all manner of places of worship are united in a common bond that is unshakable and sacred. The institutions of men are keen in causing separation by dividing "The Will of God" into contrary dogma and rhetoric, no matter the religious traditions.

This is folly in the span of the eternal. Only the truth when fully revealed in a compassionate spirit will show we are all one through God(dess). Amen.

—-

Tell me of a religious institution that is not dysfunctional, and I shall call it truly immaculate as an governing body. All institutions created by mortal hands are prone to being uneven and dysfunctional in nature. Acceptance of this sometimes selfish and competitive interests versus a cooperative spirit causes much internal conflict. Knowing this attitude is at all prevalent levels of the governing body will exercise great fortitude in its relations with all served. Such religious institutions should let go of petty motives and seek to improve all relations in an inclusive sharing spirit of open mindedness and action. So as to complete a cycle of service from the hierarchy to the end user with kindness and compassion as it's true dogma.

—-

All religions are glorified philosophies placed on a sacred pedestal of tradition. None are immune to discord from within to without of their devotees. All religions have sacred immutable truths that transcend human nature itself. It is for the wise of heart to distinguish this form of divinity from the noise and chatter of an undisciplined mind, heart, and spirit in worship. Amen.

—-

All religious institutions have become corrupted one time or another. Not by the worship of God(dess) either in singular or plural in whatever means you define and describe God. But by the controlling interests of a selfish and egoistic people. Either with misguided thinkers or worse evil plotters from within such a religious body of leaders. Spirituality is the best form of worship for an individual. Whether as a fellowship amongst others or as a solitary disciplinary practice. It is all divine no matter the path or outlet utilized to return back to the source of your creator in Heaven. Amen.

Renaissance:

For every breakthrough under the sun during an era of near limitless discoveries. One is to surmise that this period of societal development one must be living in a true renaissance. For it will be time once more that such a generation will truly wonder if they have stumbled onto the path to utopia. Those who boast that utopia is upon humanity will surely know that it is not. It is more the pride of fools leading a whole society astray and into delusion. Be wary of such spokespersons and leaders they have more up their sleeves than their idiocy.

No renaissance period can ever match the wonders and splendors of the paradise that Heaven is in God's Spirit as a whole. Those who dare speak guile will be the first ones to fall off the cliff of vanity. The rest will cherish their moment under the sun and build upon the solid ground beneath their feet. So another generation of souls will remember them and hope not to forget the combined lesson offered to all. Amen.

Revenge:

Revenge is an empty road leading no where. It is ripe with hatred and offers only destruction to its intended victim(s). It is truly one of the many inroads to perdition. Surrender such hatred with forgiveness for the sake of your own inherent sanity and well being. That is the way to reconciliation for ones own sake by mercy. Otherwise hell on Earth will persist to your own undoing. Whereby an act of revenge fulfilled is torture to one's own soul. For the sense of justification and release does not last. Only the memories of the fulfilled revenge and the initial shock of the evil done by the original aggressor becomes one twisted mess. Driving one further into insanity, where madness is no escape from the emotional and mental anguish encountered.

Rhetoric:

It has been stated that God is the one true deity and we are within his bosom of creation. Well if we as mortal beings attempt by ideology to fracture this true image of our monotheist creator by declaring this or that. We are indeed hiding if not worse distorting the divine truth from ourselves by rigid and insensible dogma. Those of stewardship and authority no matter the religious persuasion need to be on guard by not casting out the flock of God's children. Otherwise in damning others by harsh judgment led by the vanguard of the exclusive ego of a shadier spirit, then unneeded problems will persist. One will cast an equal shadow upon themselves that will need to be exercised out of their spirit by acts of purity and repentance. Amen.

Riches:

A quick rise of fame, glory, and Earthly riches equates to an even quicker fall from notoriety. Only those journeys that are gradual by moderation equate to an everlasting attainment of true riches of the Earth and of the Eternal. Of course this is mostly based on ones personal intentions whether selfish, selfless, or something entirely in between.

Righteousness:

All of God's eternal gifts be they of: love, beauty, compassion, truth, forgiveness, grace, and so forth are the seeds to the "Garden of Eden". Those who lead noble and righteous lives by moderation, which is perfection in the eyes of the Holy Spirit. Shall be whether they know it or not, become the gardeners of "Eden" the blessed horticulturalists of the soul. Amen.

--

One who seeks to prosper holistically must follow the "Will of God". Doing so will align ones self with the character of God. Journeying by such a benevolent pathway will yield sage like realizations. Of God's mighty being and all it encompasses in ones surrounding creation. Allowing oneself to dominant their personal reality by grace & wonder for the good of all. Amen.

--

One transcends this world not by ambitions of the ego. But by awakening and activating ones personal soul. By actions that are graceful and lead to a life full of hope, faith, and love. That is truly for the common good of all. Such pursuits are aided by the instruments of wisdom and virtues of character. That is the path of enlightened gratitude for ones lot in this life. Amen.

--

The power that binds us as one grand metaphysical being in the living dynamic hearth we call God. Is also the creator that liberates us to pursue our objectives, hopefully for the common good of all. With true freedom comes responsibility. However not all beings have grasped its meanings nor the implications of such a freedom. Thus chaos ensues in the universe where misdeeds occur frequently. But for those who comprehend the implications of freedom shall inherent greater powers and authority. Heaven on Earth is often the result for those that follow and live by the truth no matter where it is found. Amen.

S

Salvation:

Gaze into the holy light and that Divine Light will shine upon you the brightest. Bringing forth the graces of a good and just life to you the faithful. But, if you instead gaze into the darkness than that too will you reap in a unfortunate consequence. Of the hardships of the defeated be they lack, misery, poverty in spirit, vice, and most of all fear. Choose wisely where you place your focus in life. Otherwise your inaction will force you to make the decision for you and at times it may be the worst possible choice of all. Be vigilant and take seriously your faith in the Divine for it has saved the righteous for an eternity. Amen.

--

Those that expect God to swoop down from the heavens with his winged angels to save us from ourselves. Is grossly mistaken with that picturesque fictional interpretation. God will however by our developed Faiths transform us from within our own very being. Where humanity will serve each other and the world at large by compassion. Coming to each others aid when needed and deserved by permission. Make no mistake about this God will rescue us, but only through his creations and not outside of them. Amen.

--

Many have forgotten and few remember, but isn't that what a journey is for?

We came into this warm mortal being so that the Earth may have a tender unconditional love. All creatures have returned from paradise to be of service in this time of transition. Surrender your worries unto him who is eternal. So that your love may grow abundantly. Where such a bounty of absolute love will pour forth life in its myriad and blessed forms.

Be one with your very own "Holy Spirit". To regain what you have forgotten that is already yours to give fully. Giving in service with a joyful spirit will be your personal salvation, for now and always in eternity. Amen.

Savior:

The Lord God is our Champion & Vanguard of all that is sacred in one's life. Seek his essence always and his substance will flow through you like "Milk & Honey". To such an immense degree if allowed by your consent to bless you and your loved ones. Beyond your awareness to reach the farthest realms of the "Kingdom of God". Amen.

--

Every century nearly after the initial passing in the physical body of Jesus Christ. The masses who've revered him as a savior state he is to come back in a second coming. I say at least to myself and in solace, that the Spirit of Christ has been returning to our world constantly. Because his spirit has never left us to begin with, his grace has been here always through the "Will of God". Amen.

Scientists:

The worst thing next to a scientist that persecutes his peers, is that of an arrogant one who thwarts sensibility by their own nonchalant vanity. Such misaligned attitudes will eventually lead to the demise of their work, or worse to those who followed them earnestly at one time to do so no more. Only humility followed by honesty can heal any damage that has been rendered by their former conduct at large.

Sexuality:

Many when first exposed to sexual intimacy gain an intensified elation that through the carnal body believe to some extent that this experience in a naive fashion is love from the heart. What excludes this is if the sexual act itself was based on the vice of lust and selfish tendencies. Repeated acts of sexual intimacy beholden to those intentions will only reinforce the false nature of power over others well being.

The opposite is also true if sexual intimacy is approached from the intentions of an emotional love. Than the bonds of a Holy matrimony in a spiritual energy between the lovers will be exchanged and grow onward in progression. All acts between consenting adults be they sexual or otherwise need to be done in moderation, lest a form of gluttony develops into a obscene form of dysfunctional behavior.

If sexual development of a person is forbidden or is carried out in a gluttonous manner a schism of a persons psyche will arise. That will lead to many foul repercussions of unintended consequences that will perturb such an individual. Sexuality enacted with compassion will yield kinder results in a person's development as a mature and well adjusted individual.

Sexual intimacy is not the only vehicle for mortal affection to be displayed. It is but one of infinite outlets that unconditional love in its purity may become a channeled expression.

— —

For those that state that homosexuality is an immoral practice and sin. Are failing to recognize the inherent qualities of their personal soul or as a spirit itself. That we in the "Image of God" are transgendered or genderless souls. From God Almighty the patriarch of all creation. Is also Everlasting matriarch Goddess on the flip side of all that is feminine in qualities and archetypes. We as humanity incarnated as souls are gender neutral just like our Creator God(dess).

However our backwards mentality against homosexuality has been an affront to our very fiber of our souls in Spirit. Take responsibility of our role as souls in the "Image of God" and stop persecuting your brothers and sisters of the incarnated flesh. Otherwise you are inadvertently casting stones at yourself in that very instance because you have condemned the very essence of your soul and that of God(dess) him and herself.

Simplicity:

Simplistic solutions yield greatly expressed results. The inverse is that complicated solutions will often delay or outright offer diminished results, on any project as a whole.

--

Simplicity is a sublime ecstasy so few can cease to be captivated by her beauty. Simplicity offers so many a gentle alternative that so few can mimic. Simplicity is the daughter of wonder which flows from the mind into the beauty of all nature, whether real or fictitious.

Society:

The great pillars of a society are education, the arts, and athletics. From these three avenues of creative pursuits be they cooperative or competitive in nature. Promotes goodwill amongst your neighbors. However in such a society there needs to be the rule of law under fair and just terms of daily living. Whenever one class of people trump another than misuse and abuse will cause a society to become dysfunctional. Personal liberties must straddle the needs of the whole society, otherwise disharmony will ensue.

All societies must function with a balanced form of commerce and trade with significant oversight as to its own deliberations. If not unfair conduct will yield corruption, greed, abuse, and total incompetence. A pluralistic society needs civic participation, not just from elected officials or diplomats, but from the common ordinary citizen. All must have an emotional investment in their society lest they forget they're social responsibilities and discredit their own true value overall.

A society of peace makers must first rule themselves wisely. Before they have a true responsibility to aid other fellow societies. All societies are accountable to themselves first, otherwise a non-sustainable state of affairs will yield eventually a complete collapse of social norms.

Soul:

What we term as psychic abilities is actually a faculty of all sentient beings, no matter the scale of their physical evolution as a species. Sometimes what we term as psychic is understood in other words such as "instinct". All forms of life as we currently understand life be it in the kingdoms of: animal, insect, plant, or bacteria. Each according to there own phase of evolution each display characteristics that can be construed as instincts.

In regards to soul development of a spirit, psychic abilities are but a means to evolution of a soul. All ascended masters have showcased psychic abilities or super human feats as a manifestation of their life path. Such Masters of human benevolence are living examples of what we too can and should accomplish for ourselves and the betterment of creation as a whole.

No matter what avenue of soul development a person pursues. The highest intent based on benevolence is that of unconditional love as a catalyst force in one's soul. Be it through prayer, meditation or contemplation visualizing total unconditional love being emitted through one's third eye. Starts the process of evolving one's temperament to evolve by grace and beginning to awaken your own psychic potential literally.

Having a lifestyle of moderation of what is sacred and decent by giving of oneself. Begins again your path of all things Holy in one's present incarnation. By following your heart where it is balanced by your mind. Including always being open to the guidance of the "Holy Spirit". Will permit you to overcome many hardships and be the better for it.

Where it will eventually dawn upon your realization many beautiful truths that will wrap your heart like a warm blanket of love. We are never alone, there are always a myriad of holy companions with us. The only prerequisite is to offer your permission and surrender to the Will of God(dess) completely. That will open the doors wide for the Kingdom of God to be vibrant and alive in your personal life. Amen.

--

The only things that are real are those that are eternal. Other things be they objects or living beings may have come for a time. But a time is all that they may have by the grace of God. Many a score of such souls may have left in the physical body due to mortality. However their souls are ever present because the Spirit of God dwells upon them all. This is the grace of having lived under the supervision of all that is Holy and Sacred. Welcome this knowing and release your fears of being mortal. That the truth of your eternal soul granted by God's Spirit is real and very much alive. Amen.

Souls:

The story of our collective souls is Infinite because our maker is Infinite as well. The "Alpha & Omega" continues onward in an ascending spiral as in an unending paradox.

Our lives likewise enters one cycle and leaps onto another chain linked cycle of creation. As such it has always been a constant never ending journey thus having never begun as just mortality itself. But as an immortal extension of the same creator we call God the maker the majestic creator of all. As we are made in his / her own ethereal spiritual Image and likeness that shines with the splendor of a purpose filled Divine Life. Amen.

—

As in the Image and likeness of God our creator our Divine souls are always in Heaven. Whereas our mortal human sentient bodies are on this Earth where we all co-habitat together. How can we as children of a living creator. Be like him and have our souls abode with his Holy Spirit in Heaven?

As we are in the Image and likeness of God(dess) as souls and not just as humans. We are given this role to constantly abide with our maker in a Holy realm we call Paradise. Our souls qualify to reside in numerous dimensions at the same moment in eternity. Whereas we as humans are given the Grace through our spirits as a bridge to remember this glory once more in Creation. Amen.

—

Many have stated why are we born into corporeal form as physical beings? It is said for the purpose to grow and mature by acts of unconditional Love. As souls we are perfect due to the Image and Likeness of God(dess) within us. But as physical beings paradoxically we are flawed. It is for this purpose we are born to live and than eventually die to physical creation. This paradox of being a perfect soul and yet have a flawed physical corporeal body. Allows us as spirits to grow and mature for the common good of creation.

The womb of creation allows all life be it physical or spiritual to flourish. Without such a physical realm of creation perfect souls would have very little to keep occupied with on behalf of God's grand majestic mystery. Amen.

--

All the Gods and Goddesses of the Spirit realms be they of light or dark influences. Or the meta-deity that binds them all into one full Divine monotheist entity. Where the splendors of the Light realms are wondrous and the horrors of the dark realms are the most wicked. For both polar extremes are majestic and grandiose in scale and scope. When they as souls sojourn into physicality they both arrive as a diminutive form. Not as they are in Spirit, but paradoxically as their opposite reflection.

Christ the Savior arrives as a lowly man and becomes a carpenter by trade. But in Spirit he is the "Prince of Peace". All avatars and ascended masters amongst still others arrive into mortality as those they are meant to serve. Through most of their own nature of their realm, be it of light or darkness. Giants in Spirit are manifested as mortals of the Earth. This is the balance and the order of things in the cosmic nature of life & death eternal. Amen.

--

The essence of unconditional Love expressed in moderation that can take a soul from the "Omega" (End Point). Back to a blessed "Alpha" (New Beginning) on the behalf of grace, which is also where you already reside in the presence of God. Likewise all points of reality are simultaneously expressed in a persons soul as a complete "Circle of Life". A person's or entity's soul is a manifested non-linear expression not governed by dysfunctional thought patterns. A concurrent non-linear reality which you perceive through your state of mind. Is already intermingled within your mortal understanding of life itself.

Stop and think where you are and notice you are in a process of "soul gestation" in the womb of God(dess) always. There is thankfully no where that God is not as a reality of being, including that of your nocturnal dream state. Give yourself Peace and know all things you seek by Love Absolute (Without Conditions) will not harm you or others. But only further the goals of the "Will of God" as a blessed journey of souls. In a Holy Matrimony we all call the "Holy Spirit". Amen.

—–

The paths that a soul can take throughout eternity can be immeasurable to the naked eye. Only compassion can begin to understand this eternal journey of the soul. That can take one constantly through the totality of creation itself. As it loops beyond the scope of understanding between the realms of "Life & Death" as an ongoing cycle of rebirth. Hopefully such a soul will come to realizations of their pivotal role in life as a child of God(dess) and co-creator in life.

Where the lessons learned from one life may influence those around him or her in a manifold of blessings. This is the one eternal Love of God(dess) manifest in our hearts and for those we care for in creation. Amen.

Speech:

Praise when well deserved and sincere when offered should be accepted as an embrace of kindness. However praise when it is offered in vain by hypocrisy should be discarded immediately. When sincere criticism is expressed be open to receiving it as a teacher in disguise. When hurtful slurs are directed at you close your mind and heart from accepting them. Even if their is a portion of truth to such slurs, they not need be accepted. Due to the fact that they were delivered by a venomous poison that only conveys darkness and drowns out any semblance of truth. Amen.

Spirit of God:

The Image of God is not homogeneous as in a uniform standard. It is truly a diversified image of life in its myriad of expressions. Akin to a kaleidoscope of patterns exceeding any brilliance that an earthly rainbow can muster. God's brilliance as an entity and deity is as numerous in the Images of him or herself manifested all around us. Amen.

Spiritual Being:

Material things do not make us as persons or as a spirit. Material things are only tools for living a physical lifestyle. Be it for business or pleasure, they are a means to an end. What does make us as people or souls is our emotions, thoughts, memories, judgements, understanding, experiences, and especially our loves and fears. These are the attributes that make up a person for good or ill in this one life we're able to experience right now.

Nothing else can fully describe the sensation of life clearly enough without a dynamic and vital consciousness.

In order to appreciate all its intricacies from beginning to an end as the framework of our own unique spiritual essence. Our signature upon the Divine on us as we attempt to comprehend our own existence. Through the various religions, philosophies, or ideologies that speak loudest to us as souls. No material solution can ever satisfy such a need of identity and our role in life. Amen.

--

Why are we born into a seemingly world of chaos and disorder?

The answer can be as simple and complicated as you wish. We came back as incarnated souls so as to evolve in both the singular and plural "Spirit of God" as his entity in this version of manifested creation. Through self awareness we will grow as souls and relearn how to love all life unconditionally. Not as its master, but as its partner and friend. We can not subjugate others and not lose something Holy in the transaction. We who are reawakened by grace can choose to be better for the Holy union of God(dess) within our being. All others will need to wait a while longer in this eternal life, if they ever choose to mature and live a more wholesome lifestyle guided by the "Holy Spirit" within us all. Amen.

Striving:

We each strive for our path of salvation. Hoping by our own deeds to be a blessing to ourselves and especially to those that we love. May God keep our intentions aligned with his pure Will for our own sake by his Holy Grace. Amen.

Surrender:

Those that have great afflictions of one sort or another, are also the one's who can be the greatest healers in their own right. They just need to come to the light of tender love to release their turmoil. So as to accept all the graces that God has to offer us in an everlasting manner. This is the way to surrender our pain and to turn it into our transformation. A transformation that effects not only us, but our loved ones and those we come in contact with during the course of our lives. This is the Holy Light shining so bright that it must be shared not in haste and coercion. But gently and nurturing each other by aiding our fellows in a goodwill that transcends ideologies of exclusive membership. Come to the "Fountain of Life" drink from the eternal waters that will restore your heart, mind, and especially your spirit to all that is wholesome and holy. Amen.

--

When one longs for a release from their own heartaches and mental anguish. The simplest form of surrender is often the hardest in order to regain ones utmost composure. Where the old adage of "Let Go, and Let God" is sublime by its purest of intentions. To release your pain one must do so not with grief, but with a form of thanksgiving to God. For providing us a sacred gift as an outlet to transform or recycle our pain and return it to us as joy.

This is but one of the many roads the absolute Love of our creator God takes form in our lives. If we but permit such a grace to take hold as we surrender to his perfect Will for our own betterment or highest good. Our "Daily Bread" from the "Holy Spirit" arrives in such a form by the avenues of our spiritual heritage and kinship with the Lord

God. Relinquish your burdens unto the Lord. If your Lord is Jesus Christ bless you, if your Lord is Buddha bless you, if your Lord is Mohammed bless you, and if your Lord is Krishna bless you.

We all experience pain universally in this one life we are experiencing right now. Likewise we can experience joy in the Lord God or by the Lady Goddess if we permit grace to take hold of us in our united kinship through the "Holy Spirit". Amen.

--

Prayer, meditation, and contemplation are tools of personal surrender and worship to God. Wherein we may attune our lives as one divine being that has awakened through the glory of God within us. We may seek to lessen our pain or of the suffering of others in our worship to God. Just be mindful as we surrender, we must also surrender the outcome to the "Holy Spirit".

Demanding for this or that to occur on our own timeline is foolishness. Be still and calm by allowing the wisdom of God to flow into your mind and heart. Be detached from your own ego if wherever possible in order to recognize the good that is all around you. Doing so will foster a true sense of awe that is to be welcomed and embraced as a gift from God and his Angels. Let go of your need to control life or the life of others. For that power is beyond us to use wisely and compassionately. Be happy that you are alive and seeking to live a better life for yourself and your loved ones. Amen.

--

For those who yearn for a unity of all sorts of tender love, there you are within its wholesome embrace. None of us have left the silent, but yet powerful embrace of our creator God. It is only our ego based thinking that causes a false schism where the truth of unity is in full bloom. Surrender your false assumptions onto the "Lord God" and be set free once again in the splendor of his grand majesty in our daily lives. Doing so relives the tension in our minds and hearts allowing us to move forward. To where we need to be at that stage of our own soulful being. Let go and live deeply within the Love of God(dess) in your midst. Amen.

— —

When one's mind becomes overwhelmed and heavily burdened. Immediately stop what you were doing previously and surrender yourself to the presence of God in your midst. Seek out by simplicities sake the most comfortable spot or posture to refresh your being for that moment in time. Having achieved such a moment of inner peace, focus your senses on what is good and true by however you define such a state of mind. Then release the pressure within your mind and burden upon your heart to God(dess) unconditionally. Repeat such a surrender as many times as needed to find a tranquil space of detachment where you find yourself in your true center of being. Having rested than slowly return to your previous activity with a renewed harmony. That will gradually set you in motion to a stronger spirit filled with courage and dignity. Amen.

T

Tactics:

To be a great tactician you need a devious mind, with a dash of cunning, and a whole lot of Imagination. Not just to succeed but in order to survive to your next encounter whatever that may entail. Be sure to keep your powder dry and not lose your wits when things turn out differently than expected. Go with the flow and turn a defeat into a triumph no matter how narrow or impossible it may seem. If you are to be called a Magician than so be it and be happy to be pulling rabbits out of a hat. Than pulling something else much worse out of your own back end in fits of crazed desperation.

Talent:

I found my inner voice and I set it free. By doing so I inherently realized that we are all true expressions of the living God. By his kingdoms sake for an eternity that we sing in our own mannerisms no matter the difference of style or content. For without differing qualities Mother Nature would be sterile and very much dead without a spirit born within to showcase her infinite beauty all around. First one can only do such a thing by making a personal choice and afterwards the momentum will follow surely as one can love in their own hearts.

Teaching:

One never learns without questioning for a reason why, especially when to clarify any confusion. Fear or intimidation to question a teacher of any particular discourse is an error on the part of the student. A foreboding teacher dismantles the curiosity of any pupils so as to become an obstacle in a learning environment. Any teacher that punishes a student through mockery of a sincere question is a disruptive personality. Cutting off the hopes of any form of earnest development for the mind of the pupil to be enhanced. Acknowledging a good teacher is just as important to foster a stronger unity with the knowledge or wisdom imparted. Understanding that both the student and the teacher grow as individuals by the process of questions and answers in a shared experience is also true.

Temperament:

Those of us yearning for more life outside of us with materialistic gains will always be default fail miserably. Since trinkets, gadgets, and other do dads will only capture our interest and attention for a moment. If an addiction occurs to an external object or person then this emptiness is severely compounded by additional unwanted anxieties within.

The solution for both are to seek an inner conviction to nourish your soul with valuable content that is honest and of good cheer. This knowledge & wisdom will yield eternal, for oneself and beyond into God(dess) with much of his/her agreement.

Where such a person will be of sound mind and heart, with a glowing contentment that will have far and wide implications on one's life. Truly as an expressed grace in wonderful moderation by one's own temperament. Amen.

Transformation:

Transformation can happen unto ones self by either "Love or Fear". The imprint left behind is the most telling on a persons psyche and heart. Does one transform for the better or do they succumb to the worst possible motive. Change ushered by love and fear are both powerful forces in themselves. However love as an unconditional force has the widest and greatest impact to heal and restore. By allowing oneself always to return to their truest and wholesome Image and Likeness of God. Amen.

Traveler:

Seeing the world fully, especially as a traveler can fill one's soul with the spirit of life. By holding your "Mind & Heart" captive as its prisoner by showcasing the breath of what is possible. Be it through benevolence and hospitality for the fortunate traveler. Such a marvel of witnessing the good graces of humanity and nature herself will leave you with awe in your being. This is all the while being mindful of the inequities surrounding you be it by social or economic standing. The dignity of a good soul is a fresh and pleasant experience for both the common and extraordinary man & woman. Amen.

Trust:

Where there is trust there can not coexist any doubt. Doubt will always come undone in the majestic face of truth by default. Build on truth within yourself, and you build it in turn for those around you. Where trust will begin to sprout like the eternal gardens of God(dess). Amen.

Truth:

The only truth we keep from ourselves are the ones that truly matter. The all knowing truth of God or Life itself is open before us. What appears to be hidden or laying in secret is merely waiting for us to rediscover it for our highest good. Such an elegant expression is that of the Divine interwoven into how curious our minds and hearts can be in the search of the truth.

Not a truth that is trivial, nor one that can be replaced with another fact. But a truth that is lasting filled with meaning and purpose. That can hold steadfast in the face of conviction and not be lost in the face of liars. The truth can harm if used ruthlessly as a weapon against others. It can also soothe if used in a loving manner by wisdom to heal those that are wounded.

How you act upon the truth will be just as important as in speaking the truth before others and not bearing false witness. If your heart is filled with compassion, providence will grant you compassion as you need it abundantly. The secrets or truths of the universe lay before us to rediscover. It is only those with courage that the truth lays in wait for. All others will pass it by none the wiser. Being not concerned for the welfare of others and especially the world at large. Amen.

—–

Truth is truth, no matter the culture or society that it is shared within. The pure will heed the weight of the truth spoken no matter the setting nor circumstance. If the truth is not respected or valued. Lo, the balance will be greater than any former debts owed upon the deceivers and the deceived. For a land without truth is a land in bondage. No other form of liberty is available without the needs of a populace being met in earnest. They that keep to the darkness due to sinister motivations will suffer and perish under the weight of their own lies. Leaving only those who are righteous and of an innocent heart to proceed with dignity for the common good. Amen.

--

To understand is to allow the freedom and range of motion by one's comprehension. Understanding comes to those who are sincere in their intention to know. Such a notion of knowing must be based on a total awareness of one's motives. Otherwise a person's intent to understand is led astray or worse tricked into falsehood. To understand the truth as it presents itself is to marvel at the commonplace and sublime in one instant moment. Truth is often at a premium in a world of double standards. However it is the brightest yardstick to gauge our understanding of our world before us at large. Amen.

U

Unconditional:

Unconditional in the extreme is dangerous, unconditional in moderation is sublime. Moderation is the closest to human perceived perfection by acts done of excellence. So unconditional excellence is the path of uniform creation. Or in other words the "Eye of the Needle" as a total expression in form and action. Versus disharmonious acts done to extreme tendencies that disrupt the norm and endanger all concerned. That are expressed in absolute terms by fanaticism.

Unconditional Love:

Unconditional love is God incarnated in our lives.

--

Unconditional love is the key, the way, and the salvation. This is not some poetic musing, the energy by means of emotion we depict as love has several properties or powers. That when used in a certain way yields quantitative results of a turn for the better. In a succession of varied positive consequences. To be cherished and shared with those that are dearest to us in spirit. This is the purest outlet for the "Will of God" to take hold in our lives and the lives of many beyond us. Amen.

--

The most supreme law of God(dess) in grace is that of unconditional love. Where in love lays all the truth and beauties of the ages that the "Kingdom of God" showcases as a whole. This is a love that is many things to the infinite children of God(dess) across creation from one reality to another.

All are majestic and loved. It is up to the children of God(dess) to express such a love constantly from epoch to epoch. Doing so invites all the kindred of Heaven to join us in living our lives day to day. To triumph in the truth and the power of the one truly living and dynamic "God of gods". All else we surrender to the occurrences of the living that get miraculous glimpses of this "Great Mystery". This Love from God(dess) is both ancient and new for it is forever young by the "Will of the Holy Spirit". Know and feel this truth and it will set you free. To a life that is so richly deserved by all who know of the Love of God(dess).

— —

Unconditional Love is the great resurrection of all goodness that yields a wondrous pathway. For the seeker of that which is divine and graceful within ones self. Allowing to unfold indirectly channels for good as prosperous vehicles or inroads to be received and given akin to a full circle of life. Amen.

— —

To love oneself or another with full support even though one does not see eye to eye on many topics or ideologies. Is what is termed as unconditional love in expression and practice. As a devotion to another person where the love is its own just reward. The devotion may also encompass one's own work in recovery. From an anguish that must be observed and treated over time. In order to aid oneself in carrying one's own weight in life as a whole. Be it mourning from the grief of another passing or in treating a personal affliction whatever that may be. An unconditional Love in expression is the best course of action in the long term across an arch for the sake of doing well. Amen.

— —

Unconditional love is not just a pleasurable emotion. It is a force of the highest order of creation. This is the force many call God(dess) itself that permeates all of the (un)known realities for an eternity. So when one loves without self-imposed limits they are by such a very act invoking God(dess) into their life by willful consent. Such a invocation of pure intent enacts miracles and wonders that the agents of grace. May perform for the highest and total good for all that are open to receive such a benediction from God. So love with conditions is warped and of the human ego. Love without conditions is divine and of God(dess). Amen to the Almighty!

--

For those who lack foresight into their troubles just "Stop"! By filling yourself with the unconditional Love of God(dess). Such a love will help you transcend the emotional pain and mental anguish your encountering. By letting go of your troubles and filling your being with the Love of God(dess). We regain our true composure as a Divine being in control of our outlook on life. Allowing us to surmount any grievance whatsoever and choosing God(dess) instead as the liberating force. Once in action of such a God(dess) given grace. Life becomes manageable, sincere, and full of wonderful possibilities to grow and mature as needed. Amen to all!

--

Love is eternal just as life is unceasing throughout creation. Love may change according to the customs of displaying affection and compassion in a culture. However the meaning and substance of love remains the same no matter the age of humanity it occurs within. Know that your love is without conditions in its purest form of affection known to all creation. Amen.

--

Love unconditional is one heck of a road trip down the lanes of experience. It is never quaint nor for the faint of heart. Since only the courageous are best suited to walk in guidance within the halls of eternal Love. Others may be pretenders and speak mighty, but only the fruit of their labors shall echo the highest regard of the truth of ages. Amen.

Understanding:

To understand one must allow the richness of life and its multiplicity to be simply absorbed via your senses. Thus one opens up their "Mind's Eye" to the variety of creation itself. However with every understanding it must be done in moderation. So as to maintain an inner spirit of peace within one's own being. Otherwise ulterior ego based emotions may hijack one's own sense of justification. Surrender your need to know everything and you too will find happiness with each moment that continues to arrive. Amen.

--

So few of us have the complete honor and sacred love to explore the soul of a fellow human being. Be it as lovers, friends, or family we do not fully delve into the spiritual being of another fellow soul. The reasons are numerous however by which the main reason is we have yet to explore our own personal soul. In accordance to Socrates famous by line of "Know Thy Self" we falter as a simple and yet profound entry point. In this regard this is the "Eye of the Needle" to be threaded first before we can begin to sew. If we do not fully recognize our own souls worth. How are we to value another person or in extreme cases life itself? That is the dilemma of reaching into another persons spirit. To explore and value their soulful divinity by thoughtful and compassionate curiosity. Amen.

Unity:

The Holy Light always binds itself to its own kind, no matter the differences of nature. We are God's sacred light manifested in this world of ours, beyond the confines of mortality and physical separation. We are one because God willed it so. The ideologies that separate mortal men and woman from each other. Is the ideology of fools in the eyes of all that is Holy by the indwelling Spirit of God within us all. What humanity tears asunder, God heals over time as we surrender our will back to him in worship. Peace may not always be found in this world we call Earth. But the blessed Peace makers that live a compassionate truth are the children of Heaven where Peace reigns supreme. Amen.

Universal Law:

We are the Law of God(dess) made manifest as life itself.

Utopia:

There is no desire in Heaven, for there is no need. All of the riches of eternal creation are offered abundantly and unceasing. This is truly the utopia that all civilizations attempt to mimic themselves by example. Only a minuscule number of civilizations ever rise to such an evolutionary occasion in creation. Many more come far but fall short due to unruly ideologies and selfish egotistical demands upon the governed. When fairness trumps false wants made into needs than a society and subsequently a civilization will triumph above all. Amen.

V

Vigilance:

Those with a vigilant heart must always uphold the truth for the common good. Doing so permits transparency of the masses so as to govern with prudence and wise counsel. If the populace does not hold a government, a corporation, or any other institution in check. Than gross negligence, abuses of the system, or crimes will be committed without regard to safety, property, or the utmost general welfare for all that allows liberty to flourish.

Vigilance must occur in tandem with those who are honest brokers for the justice of the many. Otherwise there will be no accountability for the abuses or high crimes done to the State or its own citizenry. Without vigilance there is no hope for the highest good of all that are concerned for the agenda of the many. Vigilance is the sentinel of the astute and the considerate. For a place where justice is the highest and fairest regard for all who are of the "Light of God".

W

Well Being:

Beloved remember among all the hostile environments of this Earth. This one truth holds forever that a heart filled with unconditional love will invoke the "Kingdom of God" upon your shoulders. No matter what specific faith you adhere to, no exclusion can withhold the mercy & compassion of God's graces upon this truly blessed Earth. For this Earth will one day pass on as so many of her creatures have gone before her in time and space. Know that your faith guided by trust and compassion will release one from the many maladies that a mortal life can cast upon you. Be full of strength and God's courage to live wisely and full of joy. Amen.

Wickedness:

The reward for the wicked is their own undoing. They will frolic in their mischief and when payment is due they shall be bankrupt in the mind, heart, and spirit. Where balance or karma shall clear they're accounts as paid in full. The inequity caused will not only harm them, but any loved one's within their circle of contacts. Lo! Be the shame that will come down their necks and into the hearts of those closest to them. Be they friend or foe all shall see the undoing of their former ways as a cautionary tale.

Those with doubts will be made certain of the idiocy of such a fool. Step back, and catch yourself if your the fool before you fall off your own personal cliff. For your remains will be in tatters taking many years to fully recover from in sincerity. Step back, and be the wiser and follow not your ill advised comrades. Step back, and know what is decent and what is clearly not before it is too late. Amen.

Will of God:

The "Will of God" is complete for all of creation. It results always yield benevolence and grace. It is a harmonizing factor unto itself offering all a delicate balance of an inherent nature. For a person to accept the total "Will of God(dess)" for themselves grants to them a supreme recovery of well being. More than any mortal lover can complete for their own affectionate mate. The "Will of God" completes all of life unto the expressions of an absolute light guided by truth and a nurturing love. Any other will outside of that of God(dess) will lead in circles and to a loss of self. A horror no one should assume or impose on another being through deception or trickery. Amen.

—–

When one permits themselves to ardently follow the "Will of God" by a faithful devotion. This is when wonders and all manners of grace shall become self evident by the numerous daily occurrences in our lives. By invoking a glorious tradition according to the precepts of morality set throughout all benevolent humane traditions. One only becomes empowered to cross into a holy threshold of a truthful living by surrendering our ego imposed will. When such a decent lifestyle follows in the footsteps of the divine giants that came before us. This grants us the ability to transgress our flawed human nature by God's grace. Into a steadfast miraculous dynamic where our spirits become imbued in the radiance of God's mercy.

We begin to make things happen that were once uncommon to us during our normal hours. We begin to parallel the "Will of God" with those of a like mind, heart, and spirit. When we follow this "Will of God" we all celebrate in the majesty of our loving creator. Amen.

Will Power:

Where there is a will, there is always an avenue to succeed. Having a fortified will of perseverance allows a person to travel past naysayers and inner criticism. To a land of promise full of opportunity and bountiful growth to be seized and shared with many. The mother of invention grants good cheer to those who seek the fruit of their labors with an inner resolve of confidence.

Those who succumb to doubts and naysayers are broken before they have fully begun their own journey to promise and gratitude. Listen to your courage within your heart, ignore the doubts within your nagging mind of angst. Be wary of the criticism of naysayers, many have forfeited their own glories by listening to their own doubts first. The ones with strength shall overcome many obstacles before them. But know the path is not a solitary one, many true friends and helpers will be found along the way. Amen.

Wisdom:

Wisdom and knowledge gathered and not applied, is wisdom and knowledge lost on the individual. For such erudite musings of truth not used and shared freely can become a burden to any soul. One of the glories of truth is the liberation of sharing it without any form of reservations. Give and you will receive from the universe (God) without measure to no end. Such is the sacred "Will of God" become words of truth for the good life and news for all. Amen.

Wonder:

Truly living is best observed by the expressions of a childlike wonder for all creation. Such a naive wonder leads one into the purity of paradise found within themselves and that of their surrounding reality. In short childlike wonder is the purity most valued for those yearning to live again close to God. Amen.

--

Wonder is the child like place where the eternal fascination of the aged and naive stand on equal ground. Where the truth is its simplest and yet its most profound of those who gaze upon the beauty of wonder. Wonder is benevolent when the person is most humble during an encounter. Wonder transcends time with a gleeful exuberance that only the "Pure of Heart" can most appreciate and proclaim. Amen.

--

Where there is wonder there is the eye of a child filled with splendid notions. Wonder is for those who have curious hearts and a mind filled with awe. Wonder can reveal many beautiful things regarding a person. No matter their age in this life or in the next realm to come in Spirit. From young to old, those who behold wonder in their hearts shall reveal for the rest of us the glories of creation. Be it the true to the fanciful that gives delight to those who are open enough to receive such a joy. Where there is "Wonder" there is an abundant heart willingly to listen and share the beauties discovered all around themselves. Amen.

Worship:

The forms of personal worship, be they prayer, meditation, or contemplation are wonders to behold. Since they provide the grace of inner purity for one's own soul to bathe in the Holy Light of God within. Such a washing of one's spirit allows us to unfold our divinity gradually by intentions of self-betterment. Such is the path of a devout form of living by good conduct versus denying our own identity as living souls of God. Amen.

——

Physical fitness is exercise for our human bodies. Academic learning is fitness for our intellectual minds. All forms of worship by religion or spirituality is fitness for our hearts and souls. Worship of God(dess) is not just a benefit to us in a personal manner. But, also a benefit to all of creation in spirit since it spans eternity in an instant. For we are all in the "Body of God" in benefiting since true worship by grace becomes translated to all in creation as unconditional love. Amen.

——

All rituals of worship are personal and sacred between you and your Divine creator. These rituals can be dogmatic or creative in scope and in practice. As how life is both rigid and flexible according to how we view our world and how we express our love. Both the dogmatic and the creative lifestyles of worship are Holy and sacred. To say otherwise is to speak in error and to commit an unjustified slight against your neighbor. The destination to our worship is always God(dess) in totality. There is no end to how we can worship the creator of reality by unconditional love.

Paradise will always be found where our truest sense of love is to be treasured. God will grant us peace and abundance if we but withhold resentment in our hearts. Permit yourself by grace to follow such a path of righteousness not just for yourself, but for your children's peace in life. In the final analysis we live so that our next generation of worshipers may have experienced life less harshly than how we have experienced it. May these innocent souls yet to be in our fair land of creation be honored by our combined love and truly inherit paradise on Earth. Amen.

--

Do not make your spiritual faith a drudgery or that of a hardship. Keep it light and simple for that is where grace in all its wonder lays within us. This is the task of the devout in learning how to cope with life in all its intricacies and expressions. Allow the "Spirit of Hallelujah!" to take hold of you. By a means of a joy that is lived from all vantage points in this one life. Thus your comprehension by faith will grow allowing you to appreciate what is sacred not just as a witness, but as an actor of goodwill. Amen.

--

The Holy Spirit of God is a custodial being. One that nurtures without hurry those that accept his / her wondrous "Will of Testament". It is an ever loving and forgiving tranquility one is confronted by in such a sacred relationship. A solace to return to time after time in a holistic manner no matter which relationship best defines your union with the creator. So does this sacred relationship with your personal creator fill many other relationship roles as needed and sought after. The one God(dess) provides all manners of nurturing one's very own spirit. Be it a parental figure, to one of the Divine spouse, or best friend though the "Holy Spirit". All benevolent relationship roles are infinitely offered through the one God(dess) we love and worship all so dearly. Amen.

--

Prayer, meditation, and contemplation are like a boomer rang. When released truly it circles about through the "Holy Spirit". Returning back to the thrower with its resolution in hand. Surrender your requests to the "Holy Spirit". By doing so they shall circle creation in purified expressions based on spiritual truth. Allowing the majesty of God(dess) glory to shine upon it. When you are ready and open enough to receive your supplication by sacred intention. It shall bless you and your loved ones with grace of the highest orders of love. Amen.

--

To know and love God(dess) is to understand life and death itself. Both are of one act consummated in truth that frees those who comprehend this majesty of being. Albeit one does not need to know God(dess) in totality in order to experience his or her affection for all. Those of benevolence who venture into the womb of creation with earnest love in their hearts. Will yield the most bountiful harvest of their lives with absolute love as his or her own good fortune. Amen.

--

Our God is an absolute presence. So humanity may discover its own indwelling Divinity it has been blessed with by numerous faiths in our shared world. All such faiths based truly on an inclusive benevolence will lead back to the Holy Temple within your soul. Where God is awaiting us all continually throughout eternity with an unconditional abiding Love.

All faiths are relative in how they reach a state of being transcended from human form into the formless "Spirit of God(dess)" within all life. Such an awareness will nourish all hearts and minds with a tranquility that surpasses the need for understanding why. It just is the "Will of God". Be still and know this awareness of the "Spirit of God(dess)" within your being. And you to will find eternal life in abundance surrounding you constantly in both divine and human form. Amen.

Writing:

Inspirational writing and the psychic art of automatic writing are one and the same form of Divine expression. Both are connections to within the center of one's own spirit. Developed as a gift and skill simultaneously as a unified blessed form of expression. Likewise any other form of Inspirational flashes or the "Aha" phenomena is also a dynamically natural form of channeling as a psychic transmission of the soul. Stemming from the Holy collective Spirit of God which includes all Angelic Orders of a united sphere we know as the Heaven within us. We are all naturally intuitive whether we realize it or not.

Epilogue

A deep appreciation for the readers who shall take in this material and come to their own thoughtful conclusions. What it means to be a spiritual being in our day and age of globalization. This melting pot of the Earth is so varied and yet very similar in how we adore God in our personal faith traditions. May you the reader come away with a sense of being uplifted and inspired in your own faith. However you may define such a tradition of worship.

I again stand by this art form of automatic writing as the impetus of these inspirations. That come to me often as a divine muse where the angels are our spiritual relatives because we are one family under God(dess).

We are living in turbulent times that are only going to get rough. So any green pastures of nurturing our souls is gold to the person of faith no matter their age or disposition in this life. I offer the "Jewels of Truth" as a multiple volume series as a source of enrichment. As I continue to evolve as a person and especially as a soul may we all be filled with the "Holy Spirit" as instruments of a living God.

Go with God and Love everlasting. Amen.

Atrayo's Oracle

"Atrayo's Oracle" Blog Site:

Is a humble blog site for my recently posted spiritual wisdom statements. Including my other hobby of writing down futuristic abstract solutions to aspects of life that others may use at their own discretion. Copyright © 2005-2011

Web Link:

http://atrayosoracle.blogspot.com/